Hiking Waterfalls Utah

Hiking Waterfalls Utah

A Guide to the State's Best Waterfall Hikes

Stewart M. Green

FALCONGUIDES

ESSEX, CONNECTICUT

FALCONGUIDES®

An imprint of Globe Pequot, the trade division of
The Rowman & Littlefield Publishing Group, Inc.
4501 Forbes Blvd., Ste. 200
Lanham, MD 20706
www.rowman.com

Falcon and FalconGuides are registered trademarks and Make Adventure Your Story is a trademark of The Rowman & Littlefield Publishing Group, Inc.

Distributed by NATIONAL BOOK NETWORK

Photos by Stewart M. Green unless otherwise noted
Maps by Melissa Baker and The Rowman & Littlefield Publishing Group, Inc.

British Library Cataloguing in Publication Information available

Library of Congress Cataloging-in-Publication Data
Names: Green, Stewart M., author.
Title: Hiking waterfalls Utah : a guide to the state's best waterfall hikes
   / Stewart M. Green.
Description: Essex, Connecticut : Falcon Guides, [2024] | Summary: "Hiking
   Waterfalls Utah includes detailed maps and hike descriptions for 50
   easy-to-follow waterfall hikes in the state"— Provided by publisher.
Identifiers: LCCN 2023044406 (print) | LCCN 2023044407 (ebook) | ISBN
   9781493072231 (paperback) | ISBN 9781493072248 (epub)
Subjects: LCSH: Hiking—Utah—Guidebooks. | Waterfalls—Utah—Guidebooks. |
   LCGFT: Guidebooks.
Classification: LCC GV199.42.U8 G737 2024 (print) | LCC GV199.42.U8
   (ebook) | DDC 796.5109792—dc23/eng/20231016
LC record available at https://lccn.loc.gov/2023044406
LC ebook record available at https://lccn.loc.gov/2023044407

∞™ The paper used in this publication meets the minimum requirements of American National Standard for Information Sciences—Permanence of Paper for Printed Library Materials, ANSI / NISO Z39.48-1992.

Dedicated to the memory of Edward Russell Webster 1956–2022.
Longtime friend, climbing partner, fellow desert rat, Himalayan mountaineer, author
and photographer, climbing historian, father and husband, and a kind, generous,
remarkable human being. We love and miss you.
Ed, see you on the other side of the mountain.

"Davis Creek Fourth Falls" roars down a bedrock cliff, forming the best waterfall on Davis Creek.

Contents

Overview

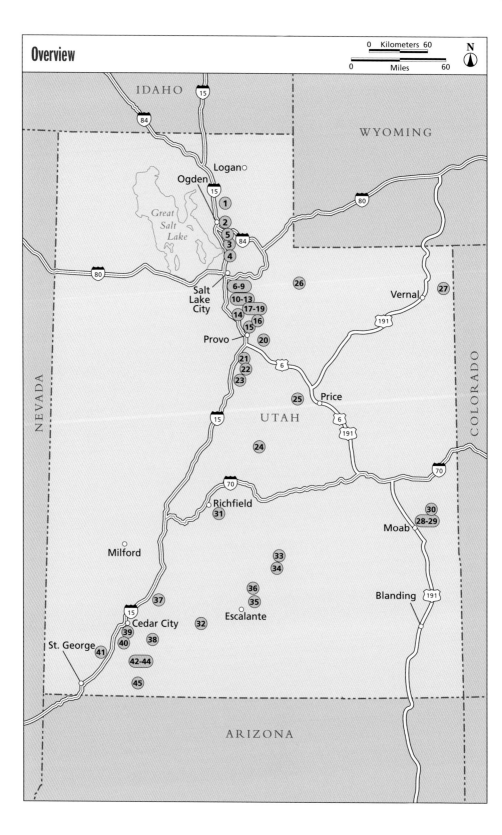

0   Kilometers   60

0   Miles   60

N

IDAHO

WYOMING

15

84

80

Logan

Ogden

15

1

Great
Salt
Lake

2

5

3

84

4

80

Salt
Lake
City

6-9

10-13

26

Vernal

27

17-19

14

16

191

15

Provo

20

21

22

6

23

25

Price

UTAH

6

191

15

24

70

70

Richfield

31

30

28-29

Moab

Milford

33

34

36

Blanding

191

37

35

15

Cedar City

32

Escalante

39

38

St. George

40

41

42-44

45

ARIZONA

NEVADA

COLORADO

Acknowledgments

Many thanks to my colleagues and friends at FalconGuides, Globe Pequot Press, Rowman & Littlefield Publishing Group, and National Book Network for their exemplary work on this exciting new book as well as the other sixty or so titles I've written for them since 1986. Also, my sincere thanks to all the bookstores and outdoor shops that carry and sell my books, providing dreams and adventures to my readers.

A special thanks to the FalconGuides staff, including acquisitions editor Mason Gadd, production editor David Bailey, cartographer Melissa Baker, copy editor Paulette Baker, proofreader Darya Crockett, and assistant marketing manager Jason Rossi. Your professional help and expertise make us authors shine!

Thanks to my good friend Max Phelps with National Book Network for supporting my books for decades and making sure they are distributed and sold far and wide on this blue planet. I appreciate your efforts and friendship.

Lastly, *muchas gracias* to Martha Morris, my partner and friend, for traveling across Utah on this amazing and memorable waterfall journey.

Meet Your Guide

Stewart M. Green has hiked, climbed, photographed, and traveled across the American West and the world in search of memorable images and experiences to document. Based in Colorado Springs, Stewart, a freelance writer and photographer for Globe Pequot Press, FalconGuides, and Every Adventure Publishing, has written and photographed over sixty-five travel and outdoor adventure books, including *Rock Climbing Utah*, *Best Climbs Moab*, *Scenic Driving Colorado*, *Scenic Driving Arizona*, *Best Hikes Albuquerque*, *Scenic Driving New England*, *Rock Climbing Europe*, and *Rock Art: The Meanings and Myths Behind Ancient Ruins in the Southwest and Beyond*. His photographs and writing are published in many magazines, books, catalogs, ads, and websites. He is currently writing a memoir of his early climbing days in Moab and Colorado and a historical novel about the Rocky Mountain gold rush.

Introduction

Welcome! A Message from Your Waterfall Guide

Welcome to the wild and wet world of Utah waterfalls! Our state, a combination of arid basins, sandstone cliffs and canyons, and skyscraping mountains, is crisscrossed by thousands of creeks, streams, and rivers. These waterways, born from mountain snowmelt and desert springs, tumble down hillsides, rest in glassy pools and reflecting lakes, and funnel through chasms, canyons, and gorges. Along the way—to the delight of the Utah hiker and waterfall lover—the water spills and splatters over crags and cliffs, splashes off boulders, and glides down granite slabs in a splendid show of waterfall wonder.

Hiking Waterfalls Utah introduces you to forty-five superb hikes to more than seventy Utah waterfalls. The treks include drive-ups to roadside waterfalls, short strolls along easy paths, moderate hikes on bumpy trails, and strenuous hikes across difficult terrain, steep slopes, and rushing creeks. This book guides you to four national forests; three national parks; two national monuments; one national conservation area; and wilderness, wildlife, conservation, and recreation areas.

The waterfall hikes lead you through a variety of ecosystems, including grasslands, meadows, dry foothills, cliff-lined sandstone canyons, montane forests filled with fir and pine, lofty subalpine zones, and spacious vistas from mountain high points. Along the trail you will see high rocky summits and clear lakes, wander through desert canyons and along slickrock rims, step through mature forests, and wade rushing rivers and chattering creeks.

On the trail you will discover a diversity of trees—bigtooth maple, blue spruce, ponderosa pine, Utah juniper, Douglas fir, lodgepole pine, Fremont cottonwood, and quaking aspen. You will hike past tall sagebrush, mats of willow, prickly pear cactus, Mormon tea, and poison ivy. A riot of colorful wildflowers adorns meadows, including cliff rose, lupine, milk vetch, columbine, fireweed, California poppy, and the elegant sego lily, Utah's state flower.

A diversity of mammals, birds, reptiles, amphibians, and fish inhabit Utah's waterfall terrain. Listen for the calls of the wild: the whir of a hummingbird, a woodpecker rat-a-tatting on a dead snag, the gobble of a wild turkey, clucks of ptarmigan at tree line, and the descending scale of a canyon wren. If you walk quietly, you will glimpse wildlife on your waterfall hike, since mule deer, elk, bighorn sheep, mountain goats, porcupines, badgers, beavers, squirrels, chipmunks, pikas, marmots, jackrabbits, bobcats, mountain lions, black bears, red foxes, coyotes, checkered whiptail lizards, rattlesnakes, and even moose inhabit the land along trails to waterfalls.

If you're adventurous, you can hike the trails alone; if you're gregarious, you can follow a trail with friends and rejoice at the sound of falling water. Depending on your fitness level, each hike can be done as a day trip, but some hikes lend themselves

to overnight backpacking or camping trips. Utah's waterfalls vary as much as the hikes that take you to them. At the end of the trail hide wilderness punchbowls and plunge pools, frothy roadside cascades, and immense cataracts that take your breath away.

But despite all the variety, Utah's waterfalls have one common denominator: how the roaring water makes you feel. Imagine plodding through thick woods and across flower-strewn meadows to a roaring creek. You follow the rush-and-tumble sound upstream along grassy banks and then hear it in the distance: the thunder of falling water. Hastening your steps, you push through willows, past aspens and firs, and then, there it is: a whitewater waterfall pouring off a granite cliff and pounding into a rock-rimmed plunge pool.

Sitting on a boulder at the base of the waterfall is restful and rejuvenating, and the flood of negative ions reduces your anxiety. You breathe deeply, filling your brain and body with oxygen, thinking great thoughts, feeling buoyant and happy, and being part of the real world, far from the madding crowd and busy streets of the place you call home. Sitting at your waterfall, soaking in silence, serenity, and elemental beauty, the place takes hold of you. Here, you think, is my real home.

Hiking Waterfalls Utah leads you across Utah's mountains, deserts, and canyons in pursuit of waterfall wonder. Enjoy the chase, look after our endangered natural places, and love the journey to these places of stunning beauty. See you on the trail!

Utah Waterfall Sources

Utah offers a magnificent landscape of startling beauty and variety. Extreme contrasts, spacious forever views, and a marvelous natural and geologic diversity that is unmatched anywhere else in the world fill the state's 89,899 square miles. The land amazes and astounds the senses with the red-rock Colorado Plateau, the skyscraping mountains in the Uinta and Wasatch Ranges, and broad basins blanketed with sagebrush. Every bend of a trail to a waterfall yields intimate glimpses into the secret heart of Utah's natural soul.

The state's rugged topography includes nineteen peaks above 13,000 feet and another seventy-three over 12,000 feet that attract wet weather in the form of deep winter snows and torrential summer thunderstorms. All that water either evaporates, absorbs into soil, or lets gravity pull it downstream. The resulting water flows make Utah a mother of rivers. Two major rivers—the Colorado and Green—slice across eastern Utah, while tributaries drain into those mighty rivers or the Great Salt Lake basin. These include the Virgin, Paria, San Juan, Escalante, Dirty Devil, San Rafael, Duchesne, Dolores, Bear, Weber, Jordan, Provo, and Sevier Rivers. Going upstream from the rivers, their headwaters fork into creeks and streams fueled by snowmelt and natural springs, providing a perfect landscape for waterfalls.

◀ *An ephemeral spring waterfall rages over a pour-off in Grand Gulch.*

Utah's mountainous geography lends itself to waterfalls, especially in the lofty glacier-carved mountains like the Wasatch Range, where you find most of the state's waterfalls, and in the arid desert regions, where steep gradients allow rain-swollen creeks to chisel sheer slot canyons through sandstone.

Most waterfalls in Utah's sandstone desert, like Zion National Park, are ephemeral and seasonal. They flow after severe summer thunderstorms that drop inches of rain in an hour in high catchment basins, pouring over towering cliffs in Zion Canyon or along Wall Street by the Colorado River outside of Moab. Be there after one of those heavy rainstorms—taking care to avoid sudden flash flooding—and marvel at the fleeting waterfall's beauty. An hour or two later, the fall stops flowing, and the rock is bone dry. This book includes no ephemeral waterfalls, since their flows are unpredictable. Instead, all the described waterfalls flow year-round, only drying up during the hottest and driest months. As in all the mountain states, May and June are the best months for chasing waterfalls.

Types of Waterfalls

The physical forms of waterfalls depend on topography and water flow, and they vary as much as the land and water that created them.

The most common type of waterfall is a **cascade**, which tumbles over rocks and boulders and down steep mountainsides, maintaining contact with the terrain. **Horsetail** waterfalls maintain some contact with the rock or earth but are more vertical and thus partially airborne. **Sheet** or **block** falls are wider than they are high, while **ribbon** falls are long and thin. **Plunge** waterfalls free-fall from cliffs, and **cataracts** are the most powerful and highest plunges. **Chute** falls shoot through narrow crevices, and **fan** falls spread their waters in fan-shaped falls. **Bridal veil** waterfalls are frothy and translucent, appearing as radiant white veils over the underlying rock face.

Waterfalls can be tiered or stepped and can stream down cliffs and crags in separate segments or serially. When low-angle or horizontal terrain like ledges stop the falling water, waterfalls often form carved punchbowls in the rock surface or plunge pools in the earth.

Waterfall types reflect the natural traits of the earth and the changeable flow of water, and as the natural world changes, so does the type of each waterfall formed. The appearance of a waterfall can change from year to year and season to season, and even from one day to the next. This is especially true during times of drought, heavy rainfall, and the annual springtime melt-off of alpine ice and snow.

When you visit a Utah waterfall, take a moment to appreciate its ever-changing beauty. You may never see that waterfall—as it appears that day—again.

Hiking Waterfalls Safety and Protocol

For your safety, the safety of other hikers, and the protection of waterfall and trail environments, follow these commonsense guidelines and etiquette when hiking to Utah's waterfalls:

- Be prepared by bringing the appropriate clothing, gear, food, water, and supplies you'll need for a safe and enjoyable hike.
- Know where you're going on your waterfall hike and have adequate directions to get there and the ability to find your way back to the trailhead.
- Share your hiking plans with a trusted friend or family member, along with the "latest time to call search and rescue," so that if you are lost or incapacitated and unable to call, your contact person can report you as missing and provide authorities with your personal details, last known location, and expected destination.
- When driving to the waterfall trailhead, be aware of changing conditions, especially during inclement weather like snowstorms or natural and human-caused disasters like wildfires.
- Rainfall, snowfall, rockfall, and wildfires can affect your travel and hiking route, so use your best judgment and be prepared to turn around if conditions become unsafe.
- Travel in small groups to lessen human impact in the backcountry. In wilderness areas, the number of people allowed to hike together on a trail is limited to fifteen.
- If you're in doubt, contact the local ranger district for directions, advisories, and road and trail closures.
- Read posted warnings and restrictions at each trailhead, as these vary between public lands and can change based on conditions. It is especially important to be mindful of campfire restrictions and required minimum camping distances from water sources. Also, remember that dogs and horses are not allowed on watershed lands in the Wasatch Range.
- Keep dogs on a leash or under voice command, and do not allow them to chase wildlife, which stresses native animals and can cause premature death.
- Do not approach wildlife. Although attacks are rare, they can happen and are more likely when an animal is provoked or feels threatened. Even small animals carry diseases, so don't try to pet or feed them.
- Beware of mountain beetle–killed trees, and never camp near them. They can fall without warning.
- Take extreme care when crossing streams, especially during spring runoff, and never wade or stand above a moving waterfall. Rocks are wet and slippery, and swift currents can quickly carry you downstream and over the edge.

- Stay clear of soft or down-sloping edges above creek beds, as well as wet, icy, or slick rocks around the waterfalls. Stick to dry, solid surfaces and avoid tragedy.
- Pack out all your trash and personal items, including toilet paper. Bury human waste, or, better yet, use a WAG bag, RESTOP, or other portable toilet kit and pack it out for proper disposal.
- Keep on established trails and avoid traveling off-trail or on social trails. When the use of side trails is required to view a waterfall, follow Leave No Trace principles to lessen your impact and prevent future resource damage. Leave No Trace (www.LNT.org) principles are easy to follow and ensure a clean and pristine environment for both wildlife and visitors to Utah's trails and waterfalls. If you do have to leave the trail, seek out hard surfaces, such as bedrock and stones, to lessen your impact.
- Leave everything on the trail as you found it. Do not remove rocks, plants, wildflowers, trees, or archaeological and historical artifacts from trails, sites, and natural areas. Leave them for other hikers to enjoy.

Wildfires and Utah's Changing Climate

Scientific studies indicate that global warming, caused by greenhouse gas emissions from the burning of fossil fuels, is changing Utah's climate. These changes include rising temperatures, decreased precipitation, lower snowpack levels, drought, an increase in insects that kill trees, increased aridification, and altered vegetation patterns. Utah's average temperature has increased by 2.5 degrees, faster than the global rise, since the early 1900s. Stream flows are predicted to decrease by as much as 15 percent by 2050, especially with decreased snowfall, since 98 percent of the water in Utah's creeks and rivers comes from snowmelt. The increasingly dry and hot conditions and an extended fire season have led to catastrophic wildfires, including the Milford Flat Fire, which burned 363,052 acres in 2007.

Hikers need to be aware of wildfire dangers when trekking in Utah's backcountry. Plan to avoid areas impacted by wildfire and smoke. Follow these basic rules to avoid wildfires:

- Before hiking, check with land management agencies like the USDA Forest Service and the Bureau of Land Management for fire restrictions in the area. Campfires may be prohibited due to red-flag fire conditions and high fire danger. Note changing fire restrictions posted on trailhead kiosks.
- Except in an emergency, do not build campfires outside of established fire rings in public campgrounds. Never leave a fire unattended, and ensure that your campfire is completely out before abandoning your campsite. Extinguish any smoldering campfires you encounter.
- Avoid hiking when the air is smoke filled and unhealthy.

- Be aware of active fires adjacent to your hiking location, even if they are miles away, and monitor their progress in case you need to change plans and return to the trailhead.
- Use extreme caution when hiking in burned forests. Dead and damaged trees create unstable terrain, and a lack of vegetation can make land prone to avalanches, rockslides, landslides, and flooding.

Reservations (May Be) Required

As of 2023, Utah is the fastest-growing state, with a 23.9 percent population increase since 2010. The burgeoning population, coupled with increased tourism, has led to overcrowding and overuse of Utah's iconic natural wonders. Increased recreational visits mean jammed roads, parking lots, trails, and trailheads; trail erosion caused by careless feet cutting switchbacks; and illegal camping and campfires.

In response, some popular Utah places have placed limitations on visitation to protect natural resources from damage caused by overuse. Zion and Arches National Parks have instituted timed-entry reservation systems, and while these systems may be an inconvenience, the benefit to visitors is a better hiking experience. Other areas require parking, camping, and hiking reservations to alleviate limited trailhead parking and damage to the area's fragile ecosystems.

Before hiking to a waterfall, especially the more popular ones, call the respective land management agency listed in the "Land status/contact" section of the chapter, or check the appendix at the end of this book for more contact information, including web addresses. Popular trailheads may require camping and hiking reservations weeks or even months in advance. Plan ahead to avoid disappointment.

Packing for Your Waterfall Hike

You'll want to dress appropriately for your waterfall hike, but there are other items you should carry for a safe and successful outing.

Start with a comfortable day pack that holds everything you need. You don't have to spend much money on a pack to satisfy your hiking needs, and you can upgrade later. Try on the pack in the store to make sure it fits your body's shape, then fill it up and see if it still feels comfortable. If waterfall hiking becomes a habit, you will wear it a lot!

Water is the most important item you carry in your pack, and how much water you need depends on your thirst and the length of the hike. You can carry water in refillable bottles or use a hydration kit like a Camelbak that allows you to sip from a tube while on the move. For extra-long hikes, carry a water filter so you can filter water from streams and stay hydrated if your supply runs out. Also bring an electrolyte drink, especially on hot days and long hikes, as your body's store of minerals quickly becomes depleted due to excessive sweating.

It is important to carry extra clothing, and that starts with a hooded rain jacket. If it rains and you get wet, you will get cold, and that will ruin your day. Also, depending on the weather, temperature, and terrain, carry extra socks; a warm knit or fleece cap; a ball cap or sun hat with a brim; gloves; a warm top layer, such as a fleece shirt; a neck gaiter, headband, scarf or "buff"; and water shoes for stream crossings to keep your hiking shoes or boots dry.

Staying warm, dry, and hydrated is important on any hike, but it's especially critical at higher altitudes and above timberline, where you are susceptible to hypothermia, dehydration, and altitude sickness. These conditions can be debilitating and deadly but are avoidable with proper planning, packing, and knowing when to turn around.

Always carry a basic first-aid kit in your hiking pack. You can buy one at pharmacies and gear shops or make your own by putting bandages, antibacterial creams, pain relievers, and other medications in a resealable plastic bag. The bag is also a good place to store a pen and paper with your personal information (including medications) and emergency contact person's information written on it.

Buy and carry a USARA (Utah Search and Rescue Assistance) card and tuck it into the first-aid kit. Purchase the card online at Rescue.utah.gov for either one or five years. Fees support a state-administered Search and Rescue fund, which reimburses costs incurred by SAR teams. The USARA card is not "rescue insurance," but it is an easy and inexpensive way for responsible hikers to support backcountry rescue personnel who may one day come to their aid.

Invest in a headlamp and extra batteries or carry a flashlight. Even the easiest trails are almost impassable in the dark, and there are no streetlights to guide you once the sun goes down. If you hike alone, carry two headlamps so you do not have to change batteries in the dark.

Buy a compass and learn how to use it. Should you get off-trail and disoriented, a map and compass—along with route-finding skills—get you back on the trail and headed in the right direction. You may want to get a GPS unit too, plus extra batteries for it. Gear shops, guide companies, and nonprofit organizations offer courses in land navigation and can provide you with the instructions you need to use these tools correctly and confidently.

Food is the best thing to carry on your waterfall hike, especially when you get to eat it! A combination of sweet and salty snacks—such as fresh or dried fruit and nuts or packaged energy bars—keep you alive and alert on the trail. For long hikes, bring lunch. Sandwiches travel well and taste great, and you can pack them in foil or plastic baggies, along with a cold pack to keep them fresh and cool. Add a bottle of your favorite beverage, like juice or an electrolyte drink in summer or a thermos filled with hot chocolate, tea, or soup in colder months.

Utah's brilliant sunny days as well as its cloudy days require sun protection. Along with a hat that shades your face, wear sunglasses, sunscreen, and lip balm, and reapply often during your hike.

Before hiking, use the toilet at the trailhead, but if you require a bathroom break along the trail, be prepared with a kit that includes toilet paper or wet wipes, plus (for women) feminine products and (for men) anti-chafing powder, cream, or stick. Double bag the kit in resealable plastic bags to keep the items fresh and dry. When you have to go, step off the trail to use them, bury all solid waste, and pack out all used items in an extra plastic bag. Many locations require that you pack out solid human waste as well, so use a WAG bag, RESTOP, or other portable toilet kit. Dispose of the used kit in a proper location at the trailhead toilets or at home.

Winter conditions demand lots of gear, including additional clothing layers, like a face mask, windproof pants and gloves, and ski goggles for extreme cold and wind; a puffy jacket to keep you warm during breaks; and microspikes or other portable traction devices that slip over your boots for safe passage on icy trails and frozen stream crossings. Some winter hikes require gaiters and snowshoes to keep your feet high and dry in deep powder.

Extra items to carry include trekking poles—especially if your hike includes elevation gain or stream crossings—bug spray, a camera, and of course a copy of *Hiking Waterfalls Utah*. Pack your guidebook in a resealable plastic baggie to keep it safe and dry for your next hike. Alternatively, copy only the pages you need and tuck them into your pocket or backpack.

Final Waterfall Hike Preparations

Now that you've selected a waterfall hike and you're packed up and ready to roll, here are more things you should know.

- Check the UDOT (Utah Department of Transportation) site at www.udot.utah. gov/connect/current-conditions/road-conditions/ for updated road conditions and closures along your travel route to the trailhead.
- Check the NOAA (National Oceanic and Atmospheric Administration) site at www.noaa.gov for weather conditions.
- Be sure that you won't be hiking through open areas and ridges or above tree line in inclement weather, especially if there's a danger of lightning. If stormy conditions arise, be prepared to descend to the trailhead immediately.
- If you plan to stay overnight at a campground, check www.recreation.gov for site availability and reservations.
- If you're traveling on snow, check the Utah Avalanche Center site at https:// utahavalanchecenter.org/ for updated avalanche conditions and areas subject to avalanche danger to avoid. A thorough discussion of avalanche safety is beyond the scope of this book, but if avalanche danger exists on your planned hike, seek the advice of an expert to determine an alternate route, choose another hike, or go another day when conditions are safer.

- Check the website of the waterfall's land management agency (see the appendix) listed in the "Land status/contact" section of each hike for notifications, updates on roads and trails, and changes in restrictions.

- In winter or spring, research the road conditions and winter gate closures near the trailhead, as roads may be impassable, closed, or gated, adding miles to your hike. Also find out about avalanche danger on the trail, and if there's a "winter route" that avoids that danger. Call the appropriate ranger station to get your questions answered before heading out.

- If you're visiting a fee area like a national park, call ahead or check online to find out how much it costs to enter. National parks and monuments, and USDA Forest Service recreation sites offer annual passes; if you plan to visit them often, it makes sense to invest in an annual or lifetime interagency pass to national parks and federal recreational lands. Purchase passes at individual parks or online. Find contact information for purchasing park passes in the appendix.

- For long drives, bring a cooler with drinks and snacks, and carry two bags for your trash: one for recycling and one for composting. Carry extra change or small bills so you can stop at local grocers or gas stations to buy snacks, drinks, or postcards and then use the restrooms.

- Plan on the drive and hike taking longer than you expect, especially if you're traveling with others. Stops for gas, snacks, and restroom breaks take time, and you should work these into your schedule. Expect them, and you won't be stressed out when they happen.

With careful planning, hiking Utah waterfalls will become a lifelong habit and your favorite part of the week. Keep the hikes fun, safe, and healthy, and you will find the sound of falling water is not only restful and rejuvenating but also good for your spirit and body. Waterfalls reduce the stress of everyday life; increase serotonin levels, which improve our moods by increasing oxygen to our brains; help us think great thoughts; and give a buoyant sense of well-being.

How to Use This Guide

Each hike includes a short overview followed by details to help you choose the best adventure for you.

Start: The starting point, usually the trailhead, for the hike.

Trail or trails: The names and numbers of trails the hike follows.

Difficulty: Refers to the level of difficulty as a guideline, as your level of fitness determines your experience.

Hiking time: The average time it takes to hike the route. The time is based on the total distance, elevation gain, trail condition, and difficulty. Your fitness level also affects your time.

Distance: The total distance of the recommended route from the trailhead back to the trailhead.

Elevation trailhead to falls viewpoint: The starting elevation at the trailhead and the ending elevation at the waterfall, along with the difference in elevation between them. This does not include the cumulative elevation gain for a round-trip hike.

Trail surface: What to expect underfoot, including dirt, gravel, boulders, or bedrock.

Restrictions: General info about fees, parking restrictions, hours, pets, camping, and other restrictions. Note that restrictions change often; contact the appropriate land management agency for details.

Amenities: Features at the trailhead and on the trail, including toilets, drinking water, visitor centers, benches, and interpretive signs.

Maps: A list of maps for the trail and trailhead, including *Benchmark Maps* (ninth edition, 2022), National Geographic Trails Illustrated maps, and USGS topo maps.

County: The county where the trail and waterfall are located.

Land status/contact: The name and phone number of the trail's land management agency. Find detailed contact info for each agency, including national parklands, national forests, and state parks, in the appendix.

Finding the trailhead: Driving directions and trailhead GPS coordinates.

The Hike: A short description of the hike.

Miles and Directions: A step-by-step guide from trailhead to waterfall, including mileage and GPS waypoints at each critical point.

Overview map: This map shows the location of each waterfall hike by hike number.

Trail maps: These maps illustrate the trailheads, access roads, trails, points of interest, waterways, landmarks, geographical features, and waterfalls.

About waterfall names: Most Utah waterfalls have unofficial names, which are enclosed in quotation marks; official waterfall names occur on US Geological Survey topographic maps and are not enclosed in quotes.

Map Legend

Municipal

≡⬡15⬡≡ Interstate Highway

≡⬡6⬡≡ US Highway

≡⬡225⬡≡ State Highway

≡⬡054⬡≡ Local/Forest Road

= = = = Unpaved Road

⊢——⊣ Railroad

-- - -- State Boundary

Trails

------ Featured Trail

- - - - - - Trail

——— Paved Trail

Water Features

◯ Body of Water

Marsh

River/Creek

Intermittent Stream

Waterfall

Land Management

National Forest / State Park

Symbols

Boat Launch

Bridge

■ Building/Point of Interest

▲ Campground

Gate

Headquarters

Inn/Lodging

Lean-To/Shelter

P Parking

Pass/Gap

▲ Peak

Picnic Area

× Point Elevation

▲ Primitive Campsite

Restroom

Scenic View/Overlook

Tower

○ Town

① Trailhead

Northern Wasatch Range

Ogden, Farmington, Layton

Filled with spring snowmelt, "Malans Falls" thunders off a vertical cliff and then spreads in a horsetail fan.

1 "North Fork Falls"

Tumbling water swirls over "North Fork Falls," a frothy cascade tucked into a hidden canyon in North Fork Park on the eastern slope of the Wasatch Range.

Start: Waterfall Trailhead
Trail: Waterfall Trail
Difficulty: Easy
Hiking time: About 1 hour
Distance: 1.6 miles out and back
Elevation trailhead to falls viewpoint: 5,830 to 6,170 feet (+340 feet)
Trail surface: Dirt, timber steps
Restrictions: Open first weekend of May to mid-Oct (weather permitting); gate hours

7 a.m. to 10 p.m. Hikers only on Waterfall Trail. No fires or firearms.
Amenities: Vault toilets at trailhead; nearby campgrounds
Maps: Benchmark Maps: Page 37 H8; Trails Illustrated #700: Ogden, Monte Cristo Range; USGS North Ogden
County: Weber
Land status/contact: Weber County Parks and Recreation, (801) 399-8230

Finding the trailhead: From I-15 in North Ogden, take exit 349 and drive east on 2700 North, which becomes 2600 North, for 4 miles to North 1050 East and turn left. Drive on North 1050 East for 0.7 mile to East 3100 North. Turn right on East 3100 North and drive east for 0.5 mile, where it turns into North Ogden Canyon Road. Follow the steep road to a pass at Ben Lomond Trailhead and descend steeply into a wide valley. After 5.2 miles reach a junction and turn left on North 3300 East. Drive north for 1.5 miles to a Y junction and keep left on North Fork Road. Drive northwest for 1.1 miles and turn left onto 5950 North, which goes to the south entrance for North Fork Park. Follow 5950 North, which becomes North Fork Park Road, and drive 1.7 miles to a T junction. Go left and drive 0.2 mile to a parking lot on the right and the trailhead. GPS: 41.371291 / -111.916485

The Hike

An unnamed creek, originating on the eastern slopes of 9,712-foot Ben Lomond, flushes down a steep canyon to 35-foot-high "North Fork Falls," a frothy cascade that empties into Cold Canyon. The off-the-beaten-track waterfall hides in North Fork Park, a 2,600-acre recreation parkland administered by Weber County Parks and Recreation on the eastern side of the Wasatch Range. The park offers 132 campsites, 6 group campgrounds, and over 27 miles on 13 trails for hikers and mountain bikers. The park is also one of nine designated International Sky Parks in Utah.

Waterfall Trail, a hikers–only trail, is a hidden gem in the northern Wasatch Mountains. The trail climbs through tall trees and a lush understory, with a nearby creek providing a symphony of rushing water. At trail's end lies noisy "North Fork Falls," splashing crystal water down a broken rock face. The waterfall is best in May and June, when snowmelt fills the creek.

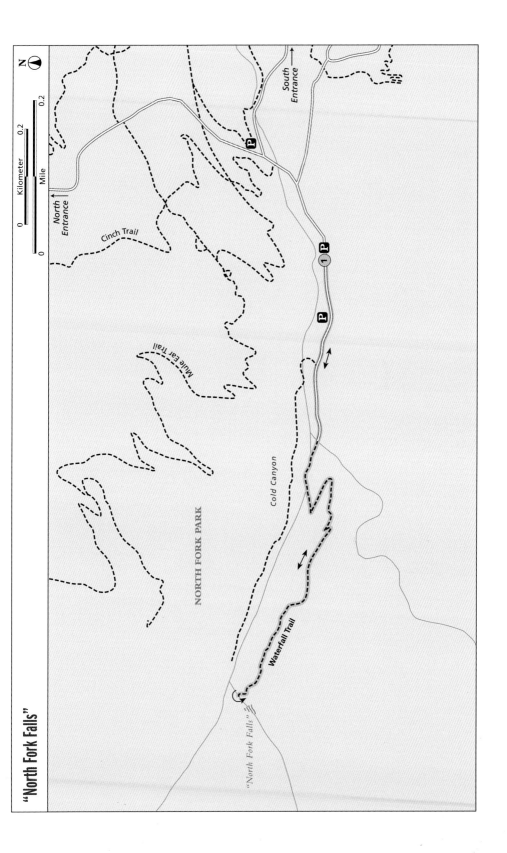

"North Fork Falls"

Waterfall Trail climbs past a creek and up wooded slopes to "North Fork Falls."

Miles and Directions

0.0   Start at the informal trailhead in the middle of the road on the west side of the parking lot. Hike up the dirt road.

0.3   Reach the road's end and an information sign (GPS: 41.371551 / -111.921479). Continue on the signed singletrack trail, making a couple switchbacks through tall trees and then hiking west through woods.

0.8   Arrive at a view of "North Fork Falls." Descend timber steps to a lower overlook near the base of the waterfall (GPS: 41.372965 / -111.927676). Retrace your steps.

1.6   Arrive back at the trailhead (GPS: 41.371291 / -111.916485).

"North Fork Falls," an off-the-beaten-track waterfall in North Fork Park, cascades 35 feet down a rocky channel.

2 "Malans Falls"

One of Utah's highest waterfalls, "Malans Falls" rumbles 305 feet off a ragged cliff in upper Waterfall Canyon, providing a wonderous display of silken water and elemental nature.

Start: 29th Street Trailhead
Trail: Waterfall Canyon Trail
Difficulty: Strenuous
Hiking time: 2–3 hours
Distance: 2.4 miles out and back
Elevation trailhead to falls viewpoint: 7,365 to 8,190 feet (+1,115 feet)
Trail surface: Dirt, gravel, rocks
Restrictions: Open 1 hour before sunrise to 1 hour after sunset. Leashed dogs allowed; immediately pick up and properly dispose of dog waste. No smoking—a smoke-free outdoor public place. No motorized vehicles and no horses. No fires or fireworks; no camping; no alcoholic beverages. Respect private property on the trail. Properly dispose of human waste and follow Leave No Trace principles.
Amenities: Restrooms and water at trailhead; services in Ogden
Maps: *Benchmark Maps:* Page 43 B9; Trails Illustrated #700: Ogden, Monte Cristo Range; USGS Ogden
County: Weber
Land status/contact: Ogden Trails Network, (801) 629-8000

Finding the trailhead: From I-15 in Ogden, take exit 341 and drive east on 31st Street for 1.1 miles; turn left (north) on Washington Boulevard. Drive 0.1 mile north on Washington and turn right (east) on 30th Street. Drive 1.4 miles to Polk Avenue and turn left. Drive north on Polk for 0.2 mile and turn right on 29th Street. Drive 0.4 mile east on 29th Street and turn right into the 29th Street trailhead (2902 Buchanan Avenue). The trailhead is on the south end of the parking lot. GPS: 41.210647 / -111.931984.

The Hike

"Malans Falls," fed by an unnamed creek that begins high on the western slope of 9,570-foot Mount Ogden, drops through Malans Basin before thundering off a huge cliff into Waterfall Canyon. The falls, measuring about 305 feet from its base to the top of its upper tier, is one of Utah's highest waterfalls. The waterfall, accessed by a good trail from Ogden, is one of the city's best hikes and iconic natural wonders. For the best waterfall views, visit "Malans Falls" in May and June, when snowmelt swells the horsetail falls. Later in summer, the creek's flow is meager but still impressive. Local ice climber Greg Lowe first climbed the waterfall in 1971, one of Utah's first major ice falls scaled in winter.

Waterfall Canyon Trail, beginning on Ogden's eastern edge, is a short, steep hike that gains more than 1,000 feet of elevation. The first trail section gently climbs into the canyon, while the second section follows the creek to the waterfall. Expect water flooding onto the trail in late spring and early summer, and plan to

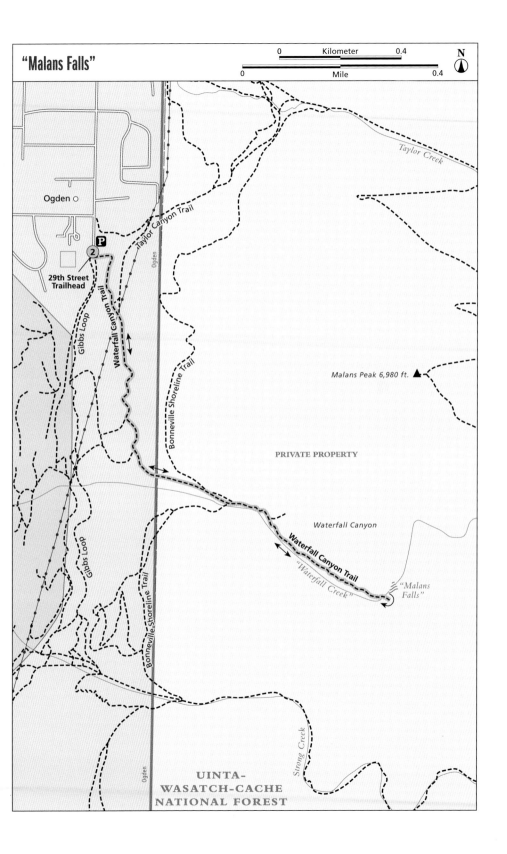

"Malans Falls"

0 — Kilometer — 0.4
0 — Mile — 0.4

N

Taylor Creek

Ogden

Taylor Canyon Trail

P
2
29th Street
Trailhead

Gibbs Loop

Waterfall Canyon Trail

Ogden

Bonneville Shoreline Trail

Malans Peak 6,980 ft.

PRIVATE PROPERTY

Waterfall Canyon

Waterfall Canyon Trail

"Waterfall Creek"

"Malans
Falls"

Gibbs Loop

Bonneville Shoreline Trail

Ogden

Strong Creek

UINTA-
WASATCH-CACHE
NATIONAL FOREST

get wet feet. Trekking poles are useful. The trail is popular with local hikers and visitors, so expect company on the trail and at the waterfall. Come during the week for more solitude.

Most of the trail and the waterfall are on private property owned by TR Guest Ranch. They allow hikers to reach "Malans Falls" on their property but ask hikers to stay on the trails, leash all dogs, pack out litter, and keep voices down so other people can enjoy the canyon and waterfall.

Miles and Directions

0.0 Start at the trailhead and walk through a pavilion to a three-way junction. Go left on Waterfall Canyon Trail, also signed for Bonneville Shoreline Trail, and climb the wide trail.

0.2 Reach a junction and go right. Follow the wide trail as it slowly ascends through scrub oak thickets. Pass a junction with a trail on the right. Continue straight.

0.3 Pass through a gate onto TR Guest Ranch property (GPS: 41.207684 / -111.930711). The ranch grants public access. Stay on the trail and avoid private property from here to the waterfall.

0.5 Continue climbing and reach a Y junction before two old water towers. Keep left on Waterfall Canyon Trail. The trail bends left and heads southeast on the north slope of Waterfall Canyon.

0.7 Reach a junction with Bonneville Shoreline Trail on the left (GPS: 41.203507 / -11.927178). Keep straight and pass a junction with Bonneville Shoreline Trail on the right after 300 feet. Continue straight and hike above the creek on the right through a canopy of trees.

0.9 Reach the edge of the creek. Hop up rocks in the creek or traverse along a low cliff on the left. The creek runs high here in May and June, so you might be wading on much of the hike from here to the falls. Continue up the creek's edge to a footbridge. Cross to the creek's south side and follow the rocky trail up steep sections, passing many frothy cascades. After the waterfall comes in view, scramble up a talus slope.

1.2 Arrive at "Malans Falls" (GPS: 41.200289 / -111.919807). Find a comfortable rock to sit on for lunch and admire the spectacular waterfall. Return down the trail.

2.4 Arrive back at the trailhead (GPS: 41.210647 / -111.931984).

"Malans Falls" pours over rock ledges in Waterfall Canyon.

3 "Farmington Creek Falls"

In the Wasatch Range west of Farmington, Farmington Creek dashes down a steep canyon to this dramatic sheet falls that splashes to a rocky creek bed surrounded by broken cliffs and thick forest.

Start: Farmington Creek Trailhead at closed Sunset Campground
Trail: Farmington Creek Trail
Difficulty: Moderate
Hiking time: About 1 hour
Distance: 1.1 miles out and back
Elevation trailhead to falls viewpoint: 6,460 to 6,095 feet (-365 feet)
Trail surface: Dirt, rocks
Restrictions: Stay on trail. Leashed dogs only; pick up after your dog. Watch for poison ivy and rattlesnakes. Skyline Drive is open year-round but may be gated closed in winter.
Amenities: None; services in Farmington
Maps: *Benchmark Maps:* Page 43 D9; Trails Illustrated #700: Ogden, Monte Cristo Range; USGS Peterson
County: Davis
Land status/contact: Uinta-Wasatch-Cache National Forest, Salt Lake Ranger District, (801) 733-2660; Farmington City Parks & Recreation, (801) 451-0953

Finding the trailhead: From I-15, take exit 395 and turn right on UT 225 East/Park Lane. Drive 0.4 mile and turn right on Main Street. Follow Main Street for 0.3 mile and turn left on 600 North. Follow 600 North for 0.1 mile until it dead-ends. Go left on 100 East, which becomes Skyline Drive. Follow paved Skyline Drive up Farmington Canyon for 1.6 miles to the Farmington Canyon Trailhead on the right. Skyline Drive becomes dirt here and begins switchbacking and edging across steep slopes on the north side of Farmington Canyon. Drive 3.6 miles up the rough road to a large pullout on the right and park. The signed trailhead is at a row of large boulders that block the former entrance to the closed Sunset Campground. GPS: 41.003337 / -111.839903

The Hike

Beginning atop Gold Ridge on the crest of the Wasatch Range, Farmington Creek rumbles down steep-walled Farmington Canyon to 40-foot "Farmington Creek Falls." The waterfall pours over a ledge, crashing onto rocks below. More cascades and small waterfalls lie farther west in the canyon.

Reach the falls by a short hike on upper Farmington Canyon Trail, which descends from Skyline Drive, a winding dirt road that runs 25 miles from Farmington to Bountiful. The trail begins at the former Sunset Campground, a forest campground that is returning to its natural state. Skyline Drive is a rough road with sharp corners, drop-offs, and narrow sections. It is passable for passenger cars most of the time, but

Hidden in a deep canyon in the Wasatch Front,
"Farmington Creek Falls" roars over a cliff.

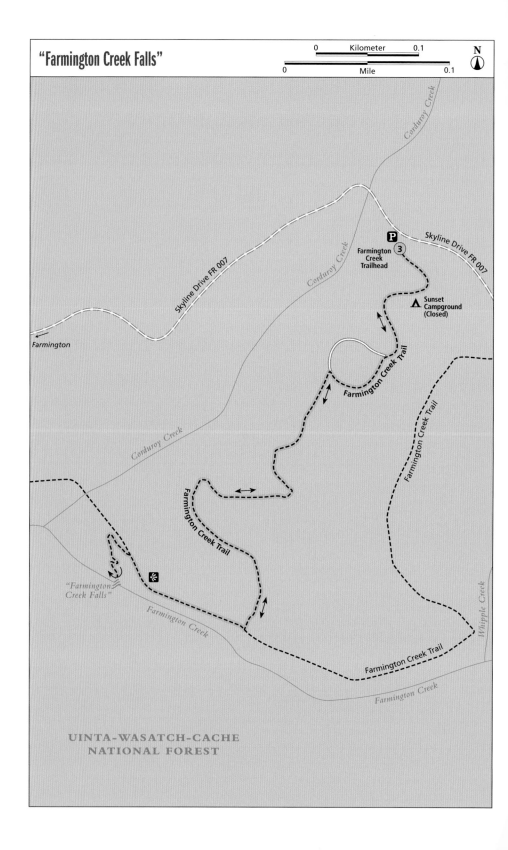

"Farmington Creek Falls"

0   Kilometer   0.1
0   Mile   0.1

N

Skyline Drive FR 007

Corduroy Creek

Corduroy Creek

P
Farmington
Creek
Trailhead

3

Skyline Drive FR 007

Sunset
Campground
(Closed)

Farmington

Farmington Creek Trail

Farmington Creek Trail

Corduroy Creek

Farmington Creek Trail

"Farmington
Creek Falls"

Farmington Creek

Whipple Creek

Farmington Creek Trail

Farmington Creek

UINTA-WASATCH-CACHE
NATIONAL FOREST

A short trail reaches spectacular "Farmington Creek Falls" in a deep canyon below Skyline Drive.

do not attempt if it is wet or snow covered. If the road is closed, park at the lower Farmington Creek Trailhead, at the end of the paved road, and hike 1.6 miles up Farmington Creek Trail to the waterfall.

Miles and Directions

0.0 Start at the trailhead signed "Farmington Creek Trail" at rocks across a closed road. Hike down the old road through closed Sunset Campground to the south end of an overgrown loop road.

0.1 Reach a trail sign (GPS: 41.002312 / -111.840687) and go south on the singletrack trail through scrub oak. Gently descend into the canyon.

0.4 Reach a T junction signed "Farmington Canyon Road." Go right on the singletrack trail and hike west through trees above the creek.

0.45 Reach an overlook of "Farmington Creek Falls" (GPS: 41.000473 / -111.842840). This is a fine view, but a tree partly obscures the falls.

0.5 Continue west on the trail to the next junction and go left. Hike down a steep, narrow trail to the edge of Farmington Creek.

0.55 Arrive at the base of "Farmington Creek Falls" (GPS: 41.000538 / -111.843195). Return up the trail to the old campground.

1.1 Arrive back at the trailhead (GPS: 41.003337 / -111.839903).

4 Davis Creek Waterfalls: "Davis Creek First Falls," "Davis Creek Slide Falls," "Davis Creek Second Falls," "Davis Creek Third Falls," "Davis Creek Fourth Falls," "Davis Creek Fifth Falls"

Crashing down a steep canyon above Farmington, Davis Creek offers more easily accessible waterfalls than any other Utah creek, with six large waterfalls and cascades as well as many smaller ones.

Start: Davis Creek Trailhead
Trail: Davis Creek Trail
Difficulty: Strenuous
Hiking time: 2–3 hours
Distance: 3.4 miles out and back to "Davis Creek Fourth Waterfall;" 3.75 miles to all waterfalls; 4.35 miles to all waterfalls and "Davis Creek Fifth Waterfall"
Elevation trailhead to falls viewpoint: 4,835 to 6,470 feet (+1,635 feet)
Trail surface: Dirt, rocks

Restrictions: Stay on trails. Leashed dogs only; pick up after your dog. Watch for poison ivy and rattlesnakes. Follow Leave No Trace principles.
Amenities: None; services in Farmington
Maps: *Benchmark Maps:* Page 43 D9, E9; Trails Illustrated #700: Ogden, Monte Cristo Range; USGS Bountiful Peak
County: Davis
Land status/contact: Uintah-Wasatch-Cache National Forest, Salt Lake Ranger District, (801) 733-2660

Finding the trailhead: From I-15 in Farmington, take exit 324 onto UT 225/Park Lane and drive east to Main Street. Turn right on Main Street; drive 1 mile south and turn right onto State Street. Drive east on State Street for 0.1 mile and keep right on UT 106/South 200 East. Drive 0.7 mile south and turn left on Woodland Drive by the Farmington City Cemetery. Continue east on Woodland Drive, which bends right and heads south. After 0.8 mile, reach the parking lot for Davis Creek Trailhead, next to a small reservoir (GPS: 40.966966 / -111.873383). Woodland Drive becomes private Little Valley Road at the parking lot. To reach the trailhead, walk 0.08 mile (430 feet) to the signed Davis Creek Trailhead on the left. GPS: 40.966020 / -111.872836

The Hike

The Davis Creek Trail in the Wasatch Range above Farmington offers one of Utah's most waterfall-rich hikes. Davis Creek, beginning on the upper west slopes of 9,259-foot Bountiful Peak, tumbles and twists down a steep canyon, pouring over six waterfalls: "Davis Creek First Falls," "Davis Creek Slide Falls," "Davis Creek Second Falls," "Davis Creek Third Falls," "Davis Creek Fourth Falls," and "Davis Creek Fifth Falls." Besides these large waterfalls, several smaller falls, including a double-drop falls at

Davis Creek Trail threads through sun-dappled bigtooth maple trees.

Indian Bathtubs, and more cascades are scattered along the creek. Like most of Utah's waterfall hikes, this memorable trek is best in May and June, when snowmelt swells the creek.

Despite being only 1.7 miles from the trailhead to "Davis Creek Fourth Falls," this is a challenging hike, with more than 1,600 feet of elevation gain. The hike's first half follows a well-signed trail past the first falls and a gorgeous slide waterfall in a steep chute to open slopes and a lush bigtooth maple forest to a pocket of tall pines called Hell Hole. From a junction here, the trail narrows, climbs steeply, and is sometimes overgrown and hard to navigate. Short side hikes to the second and third waterfalls are steep and have fixed ropes for handlines. The side trail to "Davis Creek Fourth Falls," the last described and best waterfall, is easy to miss. The last waterfall, "Davis Creek Fifth Falls," lies over a ridgeline and is an extra-credit jaunt.

Miles and Directions

0.0 Start at the signed Davis Creek Trailhead, which is 430 feet up the road from the parking lot. Hike up the trail through scrub oak groves and meadows on slopes south of the creek.

0.25 Reach a metal bench. Stop to catch your breath and look up the valley to view "Lower Davis Creek Falls," dropping through trees. Continue up the trail.

0.3 Reach a junction on the left (GPS: 40.965688 / -111.867683). This side trail jogs over to the top of "Davis Creek First Falls." Walk the shady path for about 160 feet to the waterfall, then return to the junction with Davis Creek Trail for the 0.06-mile detour.

Davis Creek Waterfalls

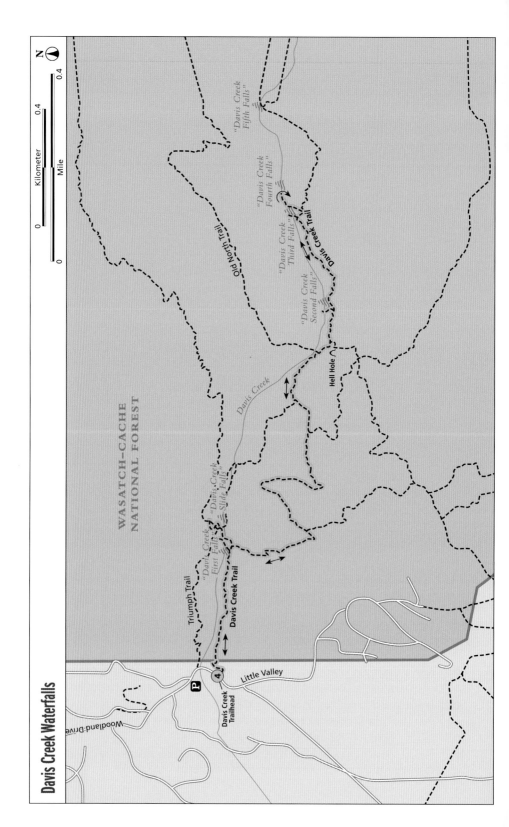

WASATCH–CACHE
NATIONAL FOREST

Triumph Trail

"Davis Creek
First Falls"

"Davis Creek
Slide Falls"

Davis Creek Trail

Davis Creek

Old North Trail

"Davis Creek
Second Falls"

"Davis Creek
Third Falls"

Davis Creek Trail

"Davis Creek
Fourth Falls"

"Davis Creek
Fifth Falls"

Hell Hole

Davis Creek Trailhead

P

4

Little Valley

Woodland Drive

N

Kilometer

0   0.4

Mile

0   0.4

"Davis Creek Slide Falls" rockets down a stone groove in a long, noisy cascade.

0.35 Turn left onto the main trail; after 50 feet, reach a signed junction (GPS: 40.965609 / -111.867524). Go right on Davis Creek Trail toward Hell Hole. The narrow trail heads south, gently climbing across an open west-facing slope.

Extra credit: To visit "Davis Creek Slide Falls," go left at a signed junction toward Triumph Trail. Walk through woods and above the creek, passing a junction for another trail to Hell Hole Camp (do not go this way), to a footbridge over the creek. Cross the creek and hike up the narrow trail to a junction. Go right and hike a steep trail to a cliff top and a view of "Davis Creek Slide Falls" in the canyon below after 0.1 mile (GPS: 40.966313 / -111.866476). Return down the trail to the bridge and back to Davis Creek Trail for a 0.2-mile side trip.

0.6 Reach a junction on the right (GPS: 40.963211 / -111.866887). Keep left on Davis Creek Trail. The right trail heads to El Capitan and Wolf Head Rock. Continue up the trail, which flattens and passes through scrub oak woods.

1.0 Reach a junction on the right (GPS: 40.963165 / -111.862860). Keep straight on the Davis Creek Trail. The right trail goes south to Prayer Rock and Cattleman Trail.

1.1 Meet a junction on the right (GPS: 40.963670 / -111.861463). Continue straight on Davis Creek Trail, bending right and passing across wooded north-facing slopes above Davis Creek. The left trail, dropping down to Triumph Trail and "Davis Creek Slide Falls," is steep, narrow, and dangerous.

1.2 Reach a junction on the left with Old North Trail. Continue straight on the main trail below tall pines.

1.25 Reach a large clearing in the trees and a major trail junction (GPS: 40.962496 / -111.859057). Go left on the trail signed "Second Waterfall." Hike across the clearing and

look right for the trail. Follow it east through trees. From the clearing, Davis Creek Trail is narrow, rustic, and may require route-finding skills.

1.3 Arrive at junction on the left, signed "Second Waterfall" (GPS: 40.962384 / -111.857887). This side trail—described on the sign, "Caution! Steep Trail! Loose Rocks! Proceed at Your Own Risk!"—descends sharply to the base of "Second Davis Creek Falls." The trail drops steeply to the base of the "Davis Creek Second Falls" (GPS: 40.962734 / -111.857786). A rope is attached to trees for the last section as a handline. Visiting the falls adds about 0.06 mile (320 feet) round-trip to the hike.

1.35 After visiting the waterfall, return to the junction and go left on Davis Creek Trail. Continue hiking to a rocky section and then traverse through tall pine trees.

1.6 Reach a junction on the left to "Third Waterfall" (GPS: 40.963583 / -111.854002). Go left and descend 80 feet down the short, steep trail, using a handline at the steepest section, to the base of "Davis Creek Third Falls" (GPS: 0.963809 / -111.853919). The short trail adds 0.03 mile to the total distance.

1.63 Afterward, climb 80 feet up to the junction and go left on Davis Canyon Trail. Follow the narrow trail up a steep ravine.

1.65 Reach a junction with a side trail on the left by a white rock outcropping (GPS: 40.963412 / -111.853724). This trail is not obvious and is overgrown in places. Turn left on the rough path, pass beneath the white boulder, and push through a scrub oak forest to a meadow with a long whitewater cascade below. Continue across the hillside.

1.7 Arrive at the base of "Davis Creek Fourth Falls" (GPS: 40.964039 / -111.853130), the best waterfall in the canyon. Eat lunch and admire the waterfall, then return down the trail.

Extra credit: Beyond the top waterfall is yet another falls—"Davis Creek Fifth Falls." Return to the junction in the ravine and go left. Climb the steep ravine and then cut left and contour across wooded slopes to a descent to the creek and waterfall. Reverse the trail back to the junction, adding another 0.6 mile to the total hike distance.

3.4 Arrive back at the trailhead (GPS: 40.966020 / -111.872836).

"Davis Creek Third Falls" crashes over rock ledges, shattering to foam and spray.

5 Adams Canyon Waterfalls: "Lower Adams Canyon Falls," "Middle Adams Canyon Falls," "Upper Adams Canyon Falls"

North Fork Holmes Creek feeds three waterfalls, including spectacular "Upper Adams Canyon Falls," in scenic Adams Canyon on the western flank of the rugged Wasatch Range above Layton.

Start: Adams Canyon Trailhead
Trail: Adams Canyon Trail
Difficulty: Moderate
Hiking time: 2–3 hours
Distance: 3.6 miles out and back
Elevation trailhead to falls viewpoint: 4,820 to 6,160 feet (+1,340 feet)
Trail surface: Dirt, rocks
Restrictions: Leashed dogs allowed. Practice Leave No Trace principles.

Amenities: Restrooms and water at trailhead; services in Ogden and Layton
Maps: *Benchmark Maps:* Page 43 C8–9; Trails Illustrated #700: Ogden, Monte Cristo Range; USGS Kaysville, Peterson
County: Davis
Land status/contact: Uinta-Wasatch-Cache National Forest, Salt Lake Ranger District, (801) 733-2660

Finding the trailhead: From I-15 in Layton, take exit 330 to Layton Parkway. Drive east for 0.1 mile to South Fork Lane and turn left. Drive north on South Fork Lane to East Gentile Street/UT 109 and turn right. Follow East Gentile Street, which becomes Oak Hill Drive, east to US 89. Cross the highway and turn left on East Side Drive for 0.1 mile to the signed parking lot for Adams Canyon Trailhead on the right, 3 miles from I-15. An overflow parking lot is on the west side of the road. The trailhead is on the south side of the main parking lot. GPS: 41.066468 / -111.909824

The Hike

Adams Canyon Trail, the most popular hike in Davis County, climbs from the eastern edge of Layton to a wooded canyon filled with the sound of tumbling cascades and three distinct waterfalls, including 45-foot-high "Upper Adams Canyon Falls." North Fork Holmes Creek, originating from springs and snowmelt on the south slopes of 9,706-foot Thurston Peak, drops sharply into Adams Canyon, where it pours over a cliff band at the upper waterfall. The two lower falls dash over boulders and rock benches between continuous whitewater cascades.

The hike, gaining almost 1,400 feet of elevation from trailhead to the upper falls, begins with switchbacks that quickly climb sunny slopes before the trail bends into

One of northern Utah's best waterfalls, "Upper Adams Canyon Falls" pours through a notch in a high cliff.

Adams Canyon Waterfalls

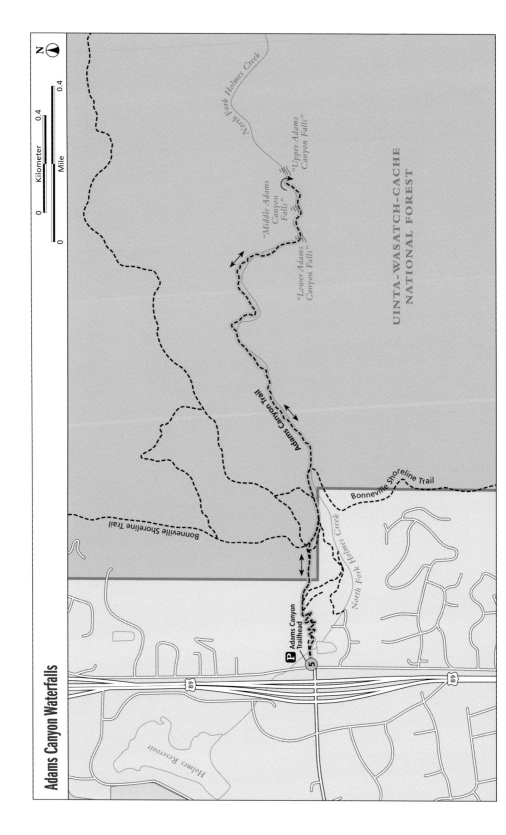

N

Kilometer
0 0.4

Mile
0 0.4

North Fork Holmes Creek

"Upper Adams Canyon Falls"

"Middle Adams Canyon Falls"

"Lower Adams Canyon Falls"

UINTA-WASATCH-CACHE
NATIONAL FOREST

Adams Canyon Trail

Bonneville Shoreline Trail

Bonneville Shoreline Trail

North Fork Holmes Creek

P Adams Canyon Trailhead

5

89

89

Holmes Reservoir

Hikers descend Adams Canyon Trail after visiting the upper waterfall.

the shaded canyon. Plan on a creek crossing on fallen logs where a footbridge washed out and wading up the creek to reach the upper falls. Use caution when crossing and wading in the creek during high water season in May and June, which is the best time to view the waterfalls. Trekking poles are useful for balance on slippery rocks.

Miles and Directions

0.0 Start at the Adams Canyon Trailhead on the south side of the parking lot. Hike east on the dirt trail next to a chain-link fence on the north side of a small reservoir. Continue up ten switchbacks on steep, sunny slopes, passing a granite marker for early settler Elias Adams and a bench.

0.3 Reach a junction with Lower Waterfall Trail on the right. Continue straight, passing another junction, and climb another hill.

0.5 Reach a junction with Bonneville Shoreline Trail on the left (GPS: 41.066406 / -111.903567). Keep right on signed Adams Canyon Trail. (Bonneville Shoreline Trail follows Adams Canyon Trail for the next leg.) Continue east on the trail, bending onto south-facing slopes in Adams Canyon.

0.7 Reach a shady junction with Bonneville Shoreline Trail above North Fork Holmes Creek. Keep left on signed Adams Canyon Trail and hike east up the canyon with the creek to your right.

1.5 Cross the creek on logs to its south bank. A footbridge here was washed out by flooding. Continue alongside the creek, which cascades over boulders. The trail becomes rough and

"Middle Adams Canyon Falls" squeezes between boulders.

rocky, crossing boulders and talus and occasionally dipping into the creek in high water. Avoid following side trails above the creek.

1.6 Pass "Lower Adams Canyon Falls" (GPS: 41.066787 / -111.886947), a 10-foot plunge waterfall and a steep cascade. Continue east along the creek's edge.

1.7 Reach "Middle Adams Canyon Falls," a smaller waterfall that pours over boulders to a noisy cascade, and hike up the narrow canyon by the creek. Before you reach the upper falls, the trail bumps against a broken cliff. Wade up the creek next to the cliff and bend right to the base of the falls. Use extreme caution wading in the creek in high water. Trekking poles are useful.

1.8 Arrive at "Upper Adams Canyon Falls" (GPS: 41.067428 / -111.885353). For good views, wade across the creek to its north bank if the water isn't too swift. After enjoying this gorgeous waterfall, return down the trail.

3.6 Arrive back at the trailhead (GPS: 41.066468 / -111.909824).

Central Wasatch Range

Salt Lake City, Sandy

High water drowns "Upper Bells Canyon Falls" during an epic runoff in 2023.

6 "Heughs Canyon Falls"

Reached by a steep trail with easy grades, "Heughs Canyon Falls" plunges through a notch in a cliff band into a shady alcove below towering Mount Olympus in the Wasatch Front east of Salt Lake City.

Start: Heughs Canyon Trailhead; begin hike from parking area on Wasatch Boulevard
Trail: Heughs Canyon Trail #1466
Difficulty: Moderate
Hiking time: About 2 hours
Distance: 3.0 miles out and back from parking area
Elevation trailhead to falls viewpoint: 4,868 feet (parking area) to 6,105 feet (+1,237 feet)
Trail surface: Dirt, rocks
Restrictions: Park only on Wasatch Boulevard at designated Heughs Canyon Trail parking.

No trail access through private property to trailhead; walk on sidewalks through neighborhood. No toilets or water at parking.
Amenities: None; services in Salt Lake City
Maps: *Benchmark Maps:* Page 43 H10; Trails Illustrated #709: Wasatch Front North; USGS Sugar House
County: Salt Lake
Land status/contact: Uinta-Wasatch-Cache National Forest, Salt Lake Ranger District, (801) 733-2660

Finding the trailhead: Reach Big Cottonwood Canyon from I-215, the beltway on the east side of Salt Lake City. From I-15 or I-80, follow I-215 and take exit 6 to 6200 South. Drive southeast for 0.7 mile on 6200 South to a left turn onto Wasatch Boulevard. Drive north on Wasatch for 0.5 mile to the Heughs Canyon Trailhead parking, a long strip of pull-in spots on the east side of Wasatch Boulevard. The start of the hike is at the north end of the parking strip at its junction with Canyon Cove Drive. GPS: 40.637216 / -111.797999)

The Hike

A sparkling creek, originating on the southern slopes of 9,026-foot Mount Olympus, drops down steep-walled Heughs Canyon to a deep notch where "Heughs Canyon Falls" tumbles over a 40-foot cliff. The lovely horsetail waterfall, tucked into a deep alcove, is the fitting climax of a steep hike up the wooded canyon from Wasatch Boulevard, on the eastern edge of Salt Lake City.

Like most of the waterfalls on the Wasatch Front, May and June offers prime viewing of "Heughs Canyon Falls," with plenty of snowmelt swelling the creek. Later in the summer the flow is reduced to a trickle. The trail is easy to follow until the last 0.1 mile, where the hike crosses a boulder field. Use your best judgment to safely cross it, watching for loose, tottering boulders.

While the Heughs Canyon Trailhead sits on the Wasatch National Forest boundary, the hike begins at a signed parking strip on the east side of Wasatch Boulevard. Hikers need to park in the designated area. Do not park in the neighborhood east of Wasatch Boulevard. Reach the trailhead by hiking 0.4 mile on sidewalks on three

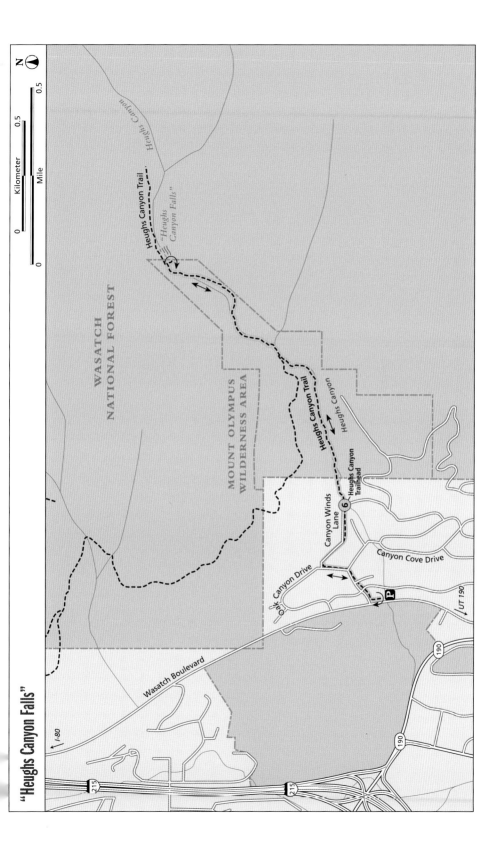

"Heughs Canyon Falls"

streets in the Cove Canyon neighborhood. When hiking up the streets, remember that this is a residential area; keep dogs leashed, stay on sidewalks as much as possible, and keep noise to a minimum.

Miles and Directions

0.0 Reach Heughs Canyon Trailhead by walking up through the Cove Canyon neighborhood. Begin at the junction of Canyon Cove Drive and Wasatch Boulevard and walk east on the sidewalk up Canyon Cove Drive.

0.1 Go left (north) on Oak Canyon Drive and walk north on the sidewalk.

0.2 Turn right on Canyon Winds Lane and pass a closed gate on its right (labeled "Pedestrian Walkway"). Walk uphill for another 0.2 mile, passing the last house at the road's end. Continue to the right of the house on a one-lane road/trail.

0.4 Reach the trailhead at the national forest boundary (GPS: 40.638422 / -111.792837). Continue northeast on singletrack trail up Heughs Canyon through dense Gambel oak thickets.

0.9 Reach a junction on the left with Bonneville Shoreline Trail (GPS: 40.641025 / -111.784815). Continue straight.

1.2 Cross the creek on a footbridge and hike north on the creek's right bank.

1.3 Cross the creek again on another footbridge and hike steeply up wooded slopes.

1.4 Reach the bottom-left side of a large boulder field that extends uphill to cliffs (GPS: 40.645937 / -111.779841). The next hike section is tricky and requires route-finding. Traverse the boulder field, taking care to avoid loose boulders and looking for places where previous hikers have stepped. On the right side of the boulders, climb down and find the trail. Follow it beneath a cliff toward the sound of falling water.

1.5 Arrive at "Heughs Canyon Falls," tucked into an alcove in a cliff (GPS: 40.645893 / -111.779355). After a picnic lunch, return down the trail.

2.6 Return to the trailhead at the end of Canyon Winds Lane. Follow Canyon Winds Lane, Oak Canyon Drive, and Canyon Cove Drive down to Wasatch Boulevard.

3.0 Arrive back at the parking area on Wasatch Boulevard (GPS: 40.637216 / -111.797999).

"Heughs Canyon Falls" spreads a lovely horsetail spray in a secluded alcove.

7 Hidden Falls

Originating in Mount Olympus Wilderness Area, Mill B North Fork drops more than 2,700 feet in a steep canyon to Hidden Falls, where it jumps through a deep notch into a cliff-walled box canyon.

Start: Mill B North Trailhead
Trails: Mill B North Trail, Hidden Falls Trail
Difficulty: Easy
Hiking time: About 30 minutes
Distance: 0.15 mile out and back
Elevation trailhead to falls viewpoint: 6,220 to 6,275 feet (+55 feet)
Trail surface: Dirt, rocks
Restrictions: Limited parking; carpool if possible; do not park illegally on the road. Salt Lake City Watershed Restrictions are strictly enforced. Dogs and domestic animals are prohibited in Big Cottonwood Canyon. This is a high crime area—do not leave valuables in your car.
Amenities: Vault toilets (seasonal) at nearby Mill B South Trailhead; services in Salt Lake City
Maps: *Benchmark Maps:* Page 43 H10; Trails Illustrated #709: Wasatch Front North; USGS Mount Aire
County: Salt Lake
Land status/contact: Uinta-Wasatch-Cache National Forest, Salt Lake Ranger District, (801) 733-2660

Finding the trailhead: Reach Big Cottonwood Canyon from I-215, the beltway on the east side of Salt Lake City. From I-15 or I-80, follow I-215 and take exit 6 to 6200 South. Drive southeast for 1.7 miles on 6200 South, which becomes Wasatch Boulevard, to a junction with Fort Union Boulevard/7200 South on the right and Big Cottonwood Canyon Road/UT 190 on the left. Turn left on Big Cottonwood Canyon Road and drive east for 4.3 miles to the S-curve, a double switchback. Park in a small lot on the inside of the top curve. Alternatively, park in a lot on the outside of the lower curve, signed "Mill B Trailhead." Begin the hike at Mill B North Trailhead, on the north side of the upper parking lot. GPS: 40.634332 / -111.724255

The Hike

Tucked into a cliff-lined cul-de-sac canyon, a short hike on two trails reaches Hidden Falls from a trailhead in the parking lot on the inside of the upper S-curve in Little Cottonwood Canyon. Hidden Falls, a frothy 45-foot chute-horsetail waterfall, is a lovely falls reached by one of the shortest hikes in this book. The best time to view Hidden Falls is in May and June.

The crux of the hike is crossing Big Cottonwood Canyon Road above the parking lot. Use extreme caution; there is no crosswalk, and the road can be busy on

Reached by a short trail at the S-curve, Hidden Falls is the most popular waterfall in Big Cottonwood Canyon.

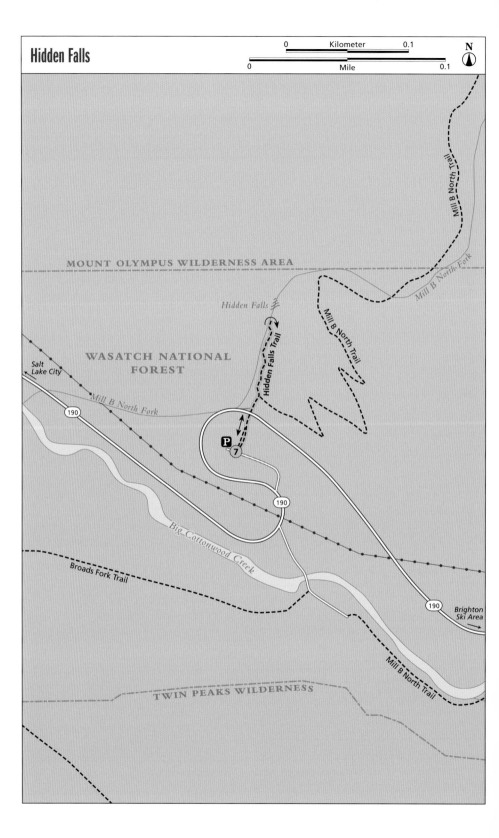

Hidden Falls

0   Kilometer   0.1

0   Mile   0.1

N

Mill B North Trail

MOUNT OLYMPUS WILDERNESS AREA

Mill B North Fork

Hidden Falls

Mill B North Trail

WASATCH NATIONAL
FOREST

Hidden Falls Trail

Salt
Lake City

Mill B North Fork

190

P
7

190

190

Big Cottonwood Creek

Broads Fork Trail

Brighton
Ski Area

Mill B North Trail

TWIN PEAKS WILDERNESS

Hidden Falls tumbles through a sharp notch in a cul-de-sac canyon.

weekends and in summer. No dogs are allowed on the trail or in Big Cottonwood Canyon, since it is part of Salt Lake City's watershed. All watershed regulations are strictly enforced. Parking can be problematic on weekends and holidays, especially in summer. If the small lot at the trailhead is full, park at the larger lot for Mill B South Trailhead at the lower S-curve. If the lots are full, park on the wide shoulder of the road, but make sure your vehicle's wheels are not on the white line at the road's edge.

Miles and Directions

0.0 Start at a two-panel sign at Mill B North Trailhead, on the parking lot's north side at the upper S-curve. Walk 80 feet up gravel and wooden steps on Mill B North Trail to the south edge of Little Cottonwood Canyon Road. Look both ways and carefully cross the busy two-lane road to its north side. Walk into the trees to a trail junction.

0.03 Reach a junction with Mill B North and Hidden Falls Trails. Go left on Hidden Falls Trail. Descend wooden stairs to Mill B North Creek and follow the trail along its east bank to a narrow cliff-lined canyon.

0.07 Reach Hidden Falls, plunging through a notch in a cliff (GPS: 40.635227 / -111.723890). It requires stepping on stones in the creek to reach the bottom of the falls. Return on the trail to the highway and parking lot.

0.15 Arrive back at the trailhead (GPS: 40.634332 / -111.724255).

8 "Moss Ledge Falls"

Elbow Fork Creek, beginning on 10,241-foot Mount Raymond, dashes down a steep canyon to a cliff band where it pours through a sheer notch, forming "Moss Ledge Falls" on the north flank of Big Cottonwood Canyon.

Start: Moss Ledge Trailhead
Trail: Moss Ledge Trail
Difficulty: Moderate, with a rock slab requiring climbing skills (Class 3)
Hiking time: 1–2 hours
Distance: 0.4 mile out and back
Elevation trailhead to falls viewpoint: 6,545 to 6,900 feet (+355 feet)
Trail surface: Dirt, rocks
Restrictions: Limited parking. Salt Lake City Watershed Restrictions are strictly enforced.

Dogs and domestic animals are prohibited in Big Cottonwood Canyon.
Amenities: None; services in Salt Lake City
Maps: Benchmark Maps: Page 43 H10; Trails Illustrated #709: Wasatch Front North; USGS Mount Aire
County: Salt Lake
Land status/contact: Uinta-Wasatch-Cache National Forest, Salt Lake Ranger District, (801) 733-2660

Finding the trailhead: Reach Big Cottonwood Canyon from I-215, the beltway on the east side of Salt Lake City. From I-15 or I-80, follow I-215 and take exit 6 to 6200 South. Drive southeast for 1.7 miles on 6200 South, which becomes Wasatch Boulevard, to a junction with Fort Union Boulevard/7200 South on the right and Big Cottonwood Canyon Road/UT 190 on the left. Turn left on Big Cottonwood Canyon Road and drive east for 5.1 miles to a parking pullout on the left (north) side of the road at milepost 7. The trailhead is on the right side of the parking area. GPS: 40.634209 / -111.711241

The Hike

"Moss Ledge Falls," a two-tiered chute and horsetail falls, is a sparkling jewel tucked into a steep canyon on the north slope of Big Cottonwood Canyon. While the hike is short, it is one of the most difficult waterfall hikes in the Wasatch Range. The trail is rocky, very steep, and difficult to follow because Elbow Fork creek is actively eroding the canyon and rockfall covers the trail in places.

Do not underestimate the difficulty and danger in reaching the falls. The hike's first crux is a slippery rock slab between towering cliffs that is climbed by using handholds and footholds. The rock is slippery, and a fall would result in injury. It is advisable to use a climbing rope to protect insecure hikers on this section both climbing up and climbing down it later. Many hikers turn around here rather than risk a fall. Another tricky section above the slab requires scrambling up loose boulders beside a tumbling cascade. Look for the best way to get up this section, but avoid climbing the cliff to the right of the creek. Use caution when descending the trail to avoid knocking loose rocks down on hikers below.

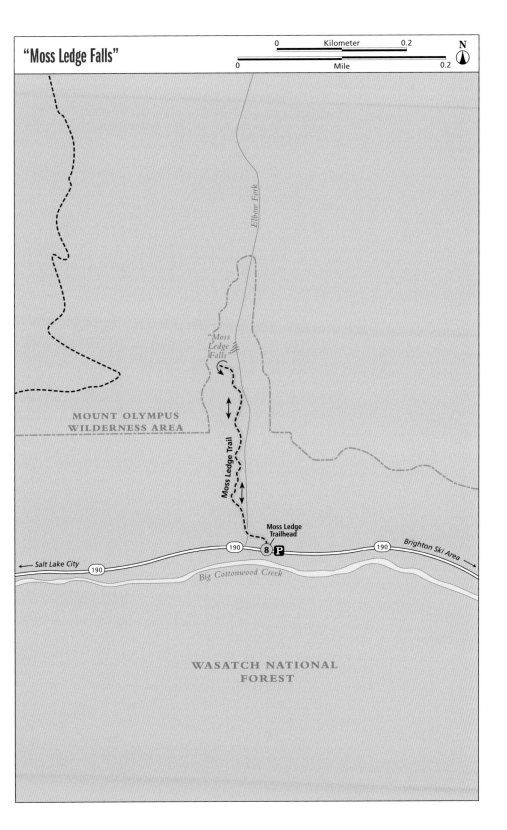

"Moss Ledge Falls"

0   Kilometer   0.2
0   Mile   0.2

N

Elbow Fork

"Moss Ledge Falls"

MOUNT OLYMPUS
WILDERNESS AREA

Moss Ledge Trail

Moss Ledge
Trailhead

190   8 P   190   Brighton Ski Area

← Salt Lake City   190

Big Cottonwood Creek

WASATCH NATIONAL
FOREST

The hike begins at an unmarked trailhead at a pullout on the north side of Big Cottonwood Canyon Road past the S-curves. The trailhead was once a national forest picnic area, but the picnic area was removed and the site restored. The waterfall's best season is June, although the creek has a good flow through the summer. It may be difficult to hike to the falls in spring, when the snowmelt-filled creek is swollen and fast.

Miles and Directions

0.0 Start at the informal Moss Ledge Trailhead, on the right side of the parking pullout. Hike up an obvious trail to a grove of tall trees, the former site of a now-rehabilitated picnic area, and Elbow Fork creek. Continue up the stony trail to the base of a 60-foot-high rock slab between two high cliffs (GPS: 40.634898 / -111.711783).

0.06 The slab is the hike's first crux—and the turnaround point for many hikers. Pick the easiest route and carefully climb the broken slab, using handholds and footholds. The rock may be slippery. Use a climbing rope if any hiker feels insecure. A small waterfall borders the left side of the slab. At the top of the slab, scramble over large boulders to another small waterfall. Climb loose rocks on the right side of this falls. Avoid climbing the larger cliff to the right. Above, follow the rocky trail up the ravine.

0.14 Reach a rockfall zone where a large cliff section fell into the canyon in 2021. Scramble over boulders and continue up the steep, rustic trail to the right of the creek.

0.2 Reach the base of two-tiered "Moss Ledge Falls," tucked into a deep notch in a cliff band (GPS: 40.636586 / -111.711972). Enjoy the sound of falling water and wildflowers growing from cracks beneath the falls. Return down the trail. Use extreme caution when descending, since loose rock abounds. Be especially careful descending the slab at the bottom of the ravine.

0.4 Arrive back at the trailhead (GPS: 40.634209 / -111.711241).

Two-tiered "Moss Ledge Falls" drops down a cliff crevice in Big Cottonwood Canyon.

9 Doughnut Falls

Fed by Mill B South Fork creek, popular Doughnut Falls gushes through a dough-nut-shaped hole at its top and then frolics down short cliffs and fallen boulders to a rocky streambed.

Start: Cardiff Fork Trailhead
Trails: Cardiff Fork Road/FR 019, Jordan Pines Connector Trail, Doughnut Falls Trail
Difficulty: Moderate
Hiking time: 2–3 hours
Distance: 3.2 miles out and back
Elevation trailhead to falls viewpoint: 6,290 to 6,800 feet (+510 feet)
Trail surface: Dirt, rocks, rock hopping in creek, pavement
Restrictions: Salt Lake City Watershed Restrictions are strictly enforced. Dogs and domestic animals are prohibited in Big Cottonwood Canyon. Do not wade or swim in the creek; do not hike up the creek above the falls. Avalanche danger at falls in winter.
Amenities: Vault toilets at main and summer trailheads; services in Sandy and Salt Lake City
Maps: *Benchmark Maps:* Page 43 H11; Trails Illustrated #709: Wasatch Front North; USGS Mount Aire
County: Salt Lake
Land status/contact: Uinta-Wasatch-Cache National Forest, Salt Lake Ranger District, (801) 733-2660

Finding the trailhead: Reach Big Cottonwood Canyon from I-215, the beltway on the east side of Salt Lake City. From I-15 or I-80, follow I-215 and take exit 6 to 6200 South. Drive southeast for 1.7 miles on 6200 South, which becomes Wasatch Boulevard, to a junction with Fort Union Boulevard/7200 South on the right and Big Cottonwood Canyon Road/UT 190 on the left. Turn left on Big Cottonwood Canyon Road and drive east for 8.9 miles to a large parking lot on the right (south) side of the road. GPS: 40.649299 / -111.648932

The Hike

A moderate hike up a well-marked trail leads from Big Cottonwood Canyon Road to Doughnut Falls, a unique cascading waterfall that features a doughnut-shaped hole at its top that Mill B South Fork pours through. View the multitiered, 100-foot waterfall from rocks and gravel bars below the falls. While the 10-foot waterfall through the doughnut hole could be seen from the base, successive rockfalls from cliffs above have choked the creek so that it is no longer viewed from below.

The popular trail is busy, especially on summer days, so plan on company both on the trail and at the falls. Plan an early morning or evening hike to avoid crowds. The national forest's summer trailhead near the end of FR 019 is best avoided, since it is usually full. The described hike does not include starting from this trailhead but from the Cardiff Fork Trailhead on Big Cottonwood Road. This trailhead offers plenty of parking and is open year-round. Access to the summer trailhead is usually open Memorial Day to late October, depending on conditions.

Doughnut Falls Trail gently climbs through aspen groves to its namesake waterfall.

The hike follows good trails with gentle grades, spectacular mountain scenery, wildflowers in summer, and a mature evergreen forest. The last hike section to the falls requires rock hopping along the edge of Mill B South Fork. Do not attempt this if the water is running high. Plan to get wet feet, because the rocks are slippery. Most hikers view Doughnut Falls from below. Seeing the doughnut hole requires scrambling during low water up large slippery rocks on the right side of the cascade. Be extremely cautious—loose rock abounds. Climb to the doughnut hole at your own risk! It is possible to follow a social trail along the west edge of the creek's inner gorge to a viewpoint above the hole.

Miles and Directions

0.0 Start at the Cardiff Fork Trailhead in the middle of the parking lot on the south side of Big Cottonwood Road (mileages start at gate across the road). Walk south on paved Cardiff Fork Road/FR 019, crossing Big Cottonwood Creek on a bridge and passing a wetland on the left.

0.1 Reach a left turn on Jordan Pines Connector Trail (also called Doughnut Falls Trail). Walk through large stones and follow the singletrack trail south through open meadows and forest clumps.

0.3 Reach paved FR 632, which leads to Jordan Pines Campground. Cross the road and hike southwest, paralleling FR 019 through the forest.

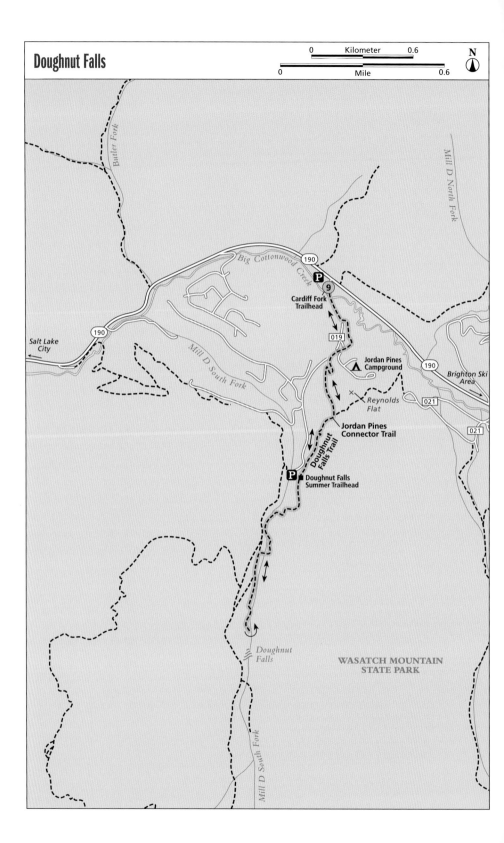

Doughnut Falls

0 — Kilometer — 0.6

0 — Mile — 0.6

N

Butler Fork

Mill D North Fork

Big Cottonwood Creek

190

P

9

Cardiff Fork
Trailhead

Salt Lake
City

190

190

019

Jordan Pines
Campground

Brighton Ski
Area

190

Reynolds
Flat

021

Jordan Pines
Connector Trail

Mill D South Fork

Doughnut
Falls Trail

021

P Doughnut Falls
Summer Trailhead

Doughnut
Falls

WASATCH MOUNTAIN
STATE PARK

Mill D South Fork

Mill B South Fork pours through a hidden hole at the top of Doughnut Falls then cascades over boulders.

0.6   Reach a junction on the left with a trail that heads east to Spruces Campground (GPS 40.642509 / -111.648693). Angle right and continue along the main trail through mature forest.

0.9   Arrive at the national forest summer trailhead for Doughnut Falls on the right (GPS: 40.639370 / -111.651043). Limited parking and vault toilets here off FR 019. Following signs for "Donut Falls," continue south on the wide Doughnut Falls Trail through meadows and forest on the left side of a broad valley.

1.3   Reach a wooden footbridge over Mill D South Fork (GPS: 40.635304 / -111.653592) and then a junction with a closed road. Go left on the trail, following the road, along the west side of the creek through meadows, aspen groves, and evergreen woods.

1.5   Reach the edge of the creek's west bank. Follow the trail along the edge of the creek's inner gorge to a broken rock section and downclimb it (a handline may be in place) to the creek. Hike and scramble up the edge of the creek, stepping on rounded boulders or wading, to a gravel terrace near the base of Doughnut Falls. Use extreme caution when wading in the creek, and do not attempt hiking upstream during spring high water.

1.6   Arrive at a good viewpoint near the base of the waterfall (GPS: 40.631144 / -111.654624). After admiring the gorgeous falls from below, return north on the trail. (**Option:** To see the actual doughnut hole, scramble up large boulders on the right side of the waterfall to the uppermost falls and the hole. Be extremely careful climbing to the hole because of slippery rock surfaces, loose rock hazards, and dangerous water.)

3.2   Arrive back at the trailhead (GPS: 40.649299 / -111.648932).

10 Lisa Falls

Reached by an easy trail, charming Lisa Falls offers plenty of oohs and aahs as it sprays down a smooth granite cliff in Little Cottonwood Canyon.

Start: Lisa Falls Trailhead
Trail: Lisa Falls Trail
Difficulty: Easy
Hiking time: About 30 minutes
Distance: 0.2 mile out and back
Elevation trailhead to falls viewpoint: 6,520 feet to 6,620 feet (+100 feet)
Trail surface: Dirt, rocks
Restrictions: Limited parking. Salt Lake City Watershed Restrictions are strictly enforced. Dogs and domestic animals are prohibited in Little Cottonwood Canyon. Watch for slick rocks, high water, and dangerous drop-offs around the waterfall.
Amenities: None; services in Sandy and Salt Lake City
Maps: *Benchmark Maps:* Page 51 A10; Trails Illustrated #709: Wasatch Front North; USGS Dromedary Peak
County: Salt Lake
Land status/contact: Uinta-Wasatch-Cache National Forest, Salt Lake Ranger District, (801) 733-2660

Finding the trailhead: From I-215 on the southwest edge of Salt Lake City, take exit 6 to 6200 South. Drive southeast for 4 miles on 6200 South, which becomes Wasatch Boulevard, to a Y junction with Wasatch Boulevard turning right. Keep straight (south) on the main road, which becomes Little Cottonwood Canyon Road/UT 210 at the junction. Follow the road, which bends east into Little Cottonwood Canyon, to a junction on the right with Little Cottonwood Road/UT 209 and a Park & Ride lot on the left. Reset your odometer here and continue on UT 210 into the canyon. From the junction, drive 2.8 miles up Little Cottonwood Canyon to a large, unsigned parking lot on the left and the Lisa Falls Trailhead. Look for the unmarked trailhead at a break in the trees. GPS: 40.572807 / -111.726490

Alternatively, reach Lisa Falls from I-15 south of Salt Lake City. Take exit 295 onto 9000 South/ UT 209. Drive east on UT 209, which becomes 9400 South and then Little Cottonwood Road, for 7.2 miles to the junction with Little Cottonwood Canyon Road/UT 210. Go right on UT 210 and drive 2.8 miles to the Lisa Falls Trailhead.

The Hike

An unnamed creek, beginning on the southern slopes of 11,330-foot Twin Peaks and 11,275-foot O'Sullivan Peaks, rockets down a steep ravine lined with granite cliffs and boulders for 4,220 feet, dropping over at least a dozen waterfalls before pouring 75 feet down a water-polished slab at Lisa Falls. A short hike on a wide trail leads from Little Cottonwood Canyon Road to the waterfall's base, offering a fun family

A popular trail leads to Lisa Falls, a dramatic horsetail waterfall below a long ravine.

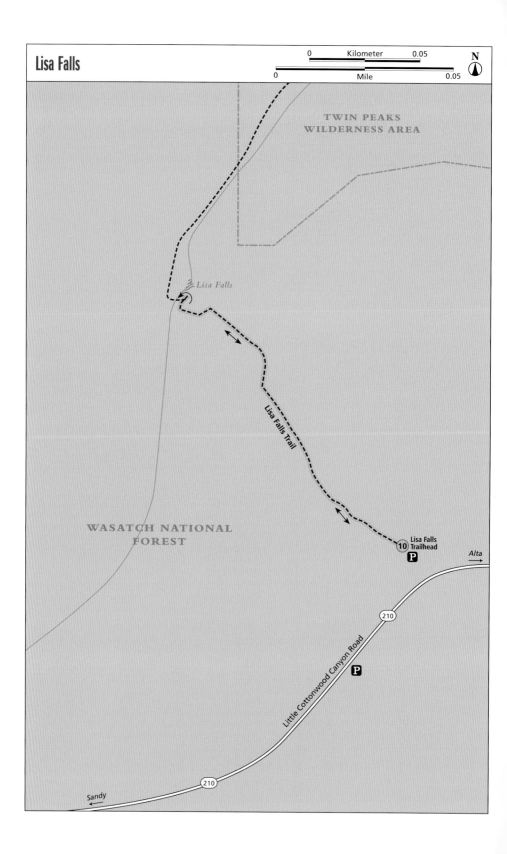

0   Kilometer   0.05

0   Mile   0.05

N

TWIN PEAKS
WILDERNESS AREA

Lisa Falls

Lisa Falls Trail

WASATCH NATIONAL
FOREST

10 Lisa Falls
    Trailhead
P

Alta

210

Little Cottonwood Canyon Road

P

210

Sandy

Rock climbers enjoy a moderate outing up slabs to the right of Lisa Falls in Little Cottonwood Canyon.

excursion on a summer day. This picturesque horsetail waterfall, gushing down a steep chute to a gravel bar, should properly be called "Lower Lisa Falls," since the USGS topo map indicates that the actual Lisa Falls is higher in the drainage.

The waterfalls above Lisa Falls are inaccessible without rock-climbing skills and gear. Do not attempt to climb the ravine; sheer cliffs, giant boulders, loose rock, and slippery bedrock are deadly problems for inexperienced scramblers. Many fatalities, mostly from falls, and injuries requiring rescue have occurred above Lisa Falls. Be safe and enjoy the waterfall from its base.

In early July 2013, a major flash flood roared down the ravine, moving boulders, uprooting trees, and reorienting the creek bed. Damage from the flood lingers at the base of Lisa Falls.

Miles and Directions

0.0 Start at the unsigned Lisa Falls Trailhead in the middle of the parking pullout. Hike north-west on a wide, rocky trail through forest.

0.1 Reach Lisa Falls below a wide granite slab (GPS: 40.573803 / -111.727651). Return down the trail to the parking lot.

0.2 Arrive back at the trailhead (GPS: 40.572807 / -111.726490).

11 "Gloria Falls"

Fed by deep snow on White Baldy in the Lone Pine Wilderness Area, White Pine Fork Creek dashes down a steep valley to "Gloria Falls," a frothy multitiered waterfall that pours over bedrock benches on the south slopes of Little Cottonwood Canyon.

Start: White Pine Trailhead
Trails: White Pine Trail #048, Red Pine Trail #050
Difficulty: Moderate
Hiking time: About 2 hours
Distance: 2.4 miles out and back
Elevation trailhead to falls viewpoint: 7,675 feet to 8,200 feet (+525 feet)
Trail surface: Dirt, rocks
Restrictions: Limited parking. Salt Lake City Watershed Restrictions are strictly enforced.

Dogs and domestic animals are prohibited in Little Cottonwood Canyon.
Amenities: Vault toilets and picnic tables at trailhead; services in Salt Lake City
Maps: *Benchmark Maps:* Page 51 A10; Trails Illustrated #709: Wasatch Front North; USGS Dromedary Peak
County: Salt Lake
Land status/contact: Uinta-Wasatch-Cache National Forest, Salt Lake Ranger District, (801) 733-2660

Finding the trailhead: From I-215 on the southwest edge of Salt Lake City, take exit 6 to 6200 South. Drive southeast for 4 miles on 6200 South, which becomes Wasatch Boulevard, to a Y junction with Wasatch Boulevard turning right. Keep straight (south) on the main road, which becomes Little Cottonwood Canyon Road/UT 210 at the junction. Follow the road, which bends east into Little Cottonwood Canyon, to a junction on the right with Little Cottonwood Road/UT 209 and a Park & Ride lot on the left. Reset your odometer here and continue along UT 210 into the canyon. From the junction, drive 5.3 miles up Little Cottonwood Canyon to a right turn to a large parking lot and the White Pine Trailhead (GPS: 40.575487 / -111.681256). The trail begins behind the toilets. If the lot is filled on busy days, park along the road.

Alternatively, reach Lisa Falls from I-15 south of Salt Lake City. Take exit 295 onto 9000 South/UT 209. Drive east on UT 209, which becomes 9400 South and then Little Cottonwood Road, for 7.2 miles to the junction with Little Cottonwood Canyon Road/UT 210. Go right on UT 210 and drive 2.8 miles to the Lisa Falls Trailhead.

The Hike

Springs and snowmelt on the northeast face of 11,231-foot White Baldy feed White Pine Fork Creek, which fills White Pine Lake and then splashes north down a steep valley to 75-foot "Gloria Falls," a multitiered waterfall, before emptying into Little Cottonwood Creek. The dramatic falls, tumbling over six distinct rock benches, is a popular summer hike for Wasatch waterfall lovers that begins at the White Pine Trailhead near Tanners Flat Campground.

Most of the hike follows easy grades up White Pine Trail, an old mining road that climbs to an alpine lake below White Baldy, before cutting off on Red Pine Trail and

White Pine Trail climbs through quaking aspens in Little Cottonwood Canyon.

finishing up an unofficial trail to the falls. The kid-friendly hike is best June through September. Midsummer hiking offers wildflowers and plenty of falling water, while autumn brings reduced flows but golden aspen groves coloring slopes along the trail. The trails are easy to follow except for the last section, which threads through tall evergreens on several social trails. Stay on the most-traveled trail to avoid further damage and minimize your impact.

Below "Gloria Falls" are several spectacular cascades. View the best cascade from a wooden footbridge on Red Pine Trail. The Red Pine Fork drainage to the west also has several unnamed waterfalls that are best viewed from Little Cottonwood Creek Road, since no trails descend into the rugged canyon below Red Pine Trail.

Miles and Directions

0.0   Begin at the White Pine Trailhead, signed for White Pine Lake and Red Lake Junction, left of toilets. Hike southwest to a left turn and continue to Little Cottonwood Creek.

0.1   Cross a sturdy footbridge over the creek to its south bank. Head southwest up an old jeep road, gently climbing through evergreen forest and aspen groves. Enjoy views of the canyon below and ragged mountain peaks.

1.0   Reach Red Pine Junction (GPS: 40.566006 / -111.689514) with a sign pointing left to White Pine Lake and right to Red Pine Lake. Go to the right of a USDA Forest Service welcome sign on Red Pine Lake Trail, a rocky singletrack trail, and head uphill.

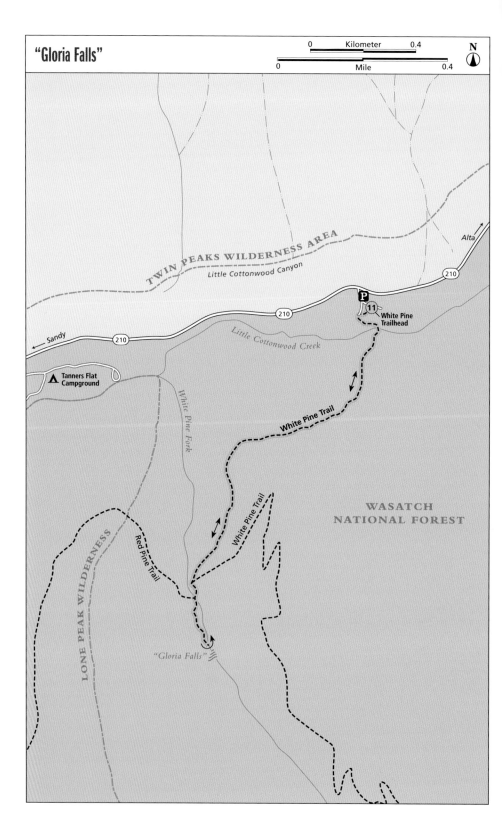

"Gloria Falls"

0   Kilometer   0.4

0   Mile   0.4

N

TWIN PEAKS WILDERNESS AREA

Little Cottonwood Canyon

Alta

210

P

11 White Pine
Trailhead

Sandy

210

210

Little Cottonwood Creek

Tanners Flat
Campground

White Pine Fork

White Pine Trail

White Pine Trail

WASATCH
NATIONAL FOREST

Red Pine Trail

LONE PEAK WILDERNESS

"Gloria Falls"

"Gloria Falls" is a popular summer waterfall above Little Cottonwood Canyon.

1.05 Reach a wooden footbridge below a frothy cascade and cross to the west bank of White Pine Fork Creek. Walk about 100 feet and go left on an unmarked trail that climbs south through tall evergreens above the rushing creek (GPS: 40.565563 / -111.689292). Follow the most-traveled trail, ignoring many social trails, to minimize your impact.

1.15 Dip down and reach the western edge of the creek. Hike along the edge of the creek to a wide rock bench below "Gloria Falls." Use caution hiking along the creek if the water is high.

1.2 Arrive at the base of "Gloria Falls" (GPS: 40.563927 / -111.688717). After enjoying the waterfall, return down the trails.

2.4 Arrive back at the trailhead (GPS: 40.575487 / -111.681256).

12 "Rocky Mouth Falls"

Tucked into a cliff-lined canyon southeast of Salt Lake City, two-tiered "Rocky Mouth Falls" squirts through a narrow gap and free-falls to a shallow pool before tumbling down a second leap.

Start: Rocky Mouth Trailhead
Trails: Rocky Mouth Falls Trail
Difficulty: Easy
Hiking time: About 1 hour
Distance: 0.8 mile out and back
Elevation trailhead to falls viewpoint: 5,115 to 5,390 feet (+275 feet)
Trail surface: Sidewalk, dirt, timber steps, rocks
Restrictions: Park only on Wasatch Boulevard at designated Rocky Mouth Trailhead parking. Open dawn to dusk; trailhead closes at 10 p.m. No access through private property to trail; respect private property; walk on sidewalks through neighborhood. No toilets or water at parking. Stay on the trail. No alcoholic beverages. The creek is in the Wasatch Front Watershed; restrictions are strictly enforced. Dogs prohibited in Rocky Mouth Canyon. Watch for slick rocks, high water, and dangerous drop-offs above the waterfall.
Amenities: None; services in Salt Lake City
Maps: *Benchmark Maps:* Page 51 A9; Trails Illustrated #709: Wasatch Front North; USGS Draper
County: Salt Lake
Land status/contact: Uinta-Wasatch-Cache National Forest, Salt Lake Ranger District, (801) 733-2660

Finding the trailhead: From I-215 on the southwest edge of Salt Lake City, take exit 6 to 6200 South. Drive southeast for 4 miles on 6200 South, which becomes Wasatch Boulevard, to a Y junction with Wasatch Boulevard turning right and Little Cottonwood Canyon Road/UT 210 going straight. Turn right on Wasatch and drive south for 3.2 miles to the Rocky Mouth Trailhead and parking lot on the left (GPS: 40.547155 / -111.806356). Trailhead address: 11248 Wasatch Blvd., Sandy.

Alternatively, reach "Rocky Mouth Falls" from I-15 south of Salt Lake City. Take exit 295 onto 9000 South/UT 209. Drive east on UT 209, which becomes 9400 South and then Little Cottonwood Road, for 5.9 miles to the junction with Wasatch Boulevard. Go right on Wasatch and drive 2.1 miles south to the Rocky Mouth Trailhead.

The Hike

Hidden among cliffs in the aptly named Rocky Mouth Canyon, 70-foot "Rocky Mouth Falls" is an easily accessible horsetail waterfall on the eastern edge of suburban Sandy, southeast of Salt Lake City. Visit the waterfall, fed by springs and snowmelt

"Rocky Mouth Falls" tucks into a hidden canyon in the
Wasatch Range above Sandy.

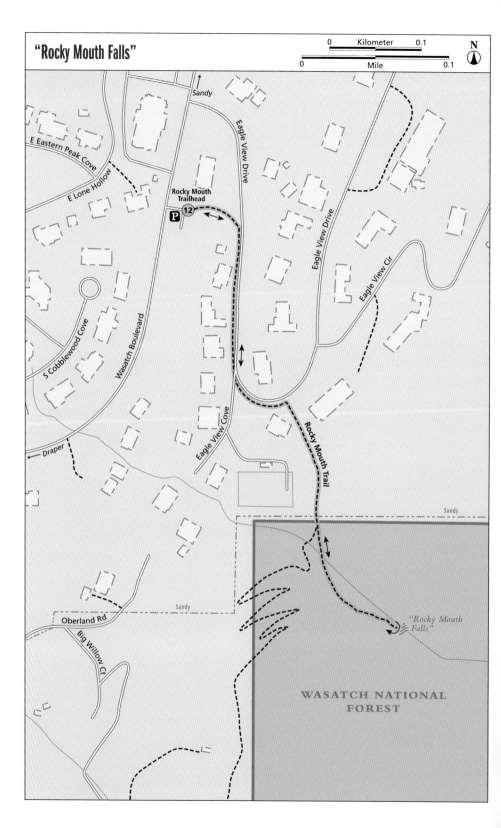

"Rocky Mouth Falls"

0   Kilometer   0.1

0   Mile   0.1

N

Sandy

E Eastern Peak Cove

E Lone Hollow

Eagle View Drive

Rocky Mouth Trailhead

P   12

Eagle View Drive

Eagle View Cir

S Cobblewood Cove

Wasatch Boulevard

Draper

Eagle View Cove

Rocky Mouth Trail

Sandy

Oberland Rd

Sandy

Big Willow Ct

"Rocky Mouth Falls"

WASATCH NATIONAL FOREST

from high peaks in the Lone Pine Wilderness Area, in late spring and early summer for the best views. The waterfall's flow depletes to a trickle by late August.

Access the short, family-friendly trail from a designated parking lot on Wasatch Boulevard south of Little Cottonwood Canyon. The hike's first section climbs timber steps to Eagle View Drive and a ritzy neighborhood. To preserve waterfall access, it is important to avoid trespassing on private property and to follow the sidewalk alongside the road to the trailhead, a gate between high fences. The trail and waterfall are often busy, especially on hot days, when locals hike to the falls to cool off. Remember to leave your dog behind, since the area lies in the Wasatch Front Watershed.

Miles and Directions

0.0   Start at the signed Rocky Mouth Trailhead at the north end of the parking lot on Wasatch Boulevard. Walk past signs explaining the watershed and trail rules, then climb a long set of timber stairs for 200 feet to Eagle View Drive. Go right on the sidewalk and follow signs to the trail.

0.2   Reach the Rocky Mouth Trailhead at a gate and sign (GPS: 40.545329 / -111.805112). Hike up the narrow trail, flanked by fences between houses, and climb timber steps.

0.3   Reach a Y junction and keep left, following a sign for the falls. The trail reaches the creek and bends left, climbing through thick forest and over rocks.

0.4   Arrive at "Rocky Mouth Falls" (GPS: 40.543178 / -111.803660). Return down the trail to the trailhead and Eagle View Drive. Go left and follow the sidewalk back to the steps down to Wasatch Boulevard.

0.8   Arrive back at the trailhead (GPS: 40.547155 / -111.806356).

13 Bells Canyon Waterfalls : "Lower Bells Canyon Falls," "Upper Bells Canyon Falls"

In a high valley in the Lone Peak Wilderness Area, two spectacular waterfalls—"Lower Bells Canyon Falls" and "Upper Bells Canyon Falls"—plunge off granite cliffs in shimmering sprays of translucent water.

Start: Bells Canyon Preservation Trailhead
Trail: Bell Canyon Trail
Difficulty: Moderate
Hiking time: 3–4 hours
Distance: 5.6 miles out and back to upper falls; 4.5 miles out and back to lower falls
Elevation trailhead to falls viewpoint: 5,310 to 7,470 feet (+2,160 feet)
Trail surface: Dirt, rocks
Restrictions: Trailhead hours sunrise to 10 p.m. No dogs; no swimming, camping, campfires, fireworks, or horses. Pack out your trash; pick up litter; pack out human waste, and use a WAG bag, RESTOP, or other portable toilet kit. Practice Leave No Trace principles.
Amenities: Restrooms, drinking water, benches, picnic tables, interpretive signs at trailhead; services in Sandy and Salt Lake City
Maps: *Benchmark Maps:* Page 51 A10; Trails Illustrated #709: Wasatch Front North; USGS Draper, Dromedary Peak
County: Salt Lake
Land status/contact: Uinta-Wasatch-Cache National Forest, Salt Lake Ranger District, (801) 733-2660; Sandy Park and Recreation, (801) 568-2900

Finding the trailhead: From I-215 on the southwest edge of Salt Lake City, take exit 6 to 6200 South. Drive southeast for 4 miles on 6200 South, which becomes Wasatch Boulevard, to a Y junction with Wasatch Boulevard turning right and Little Cottonwood Canyon Road/UT 210 going straight. Turn right on Wasatch and drive south for 1.3 miles to a signed left turn on a road that leads 0.3 mile to a large parking lot and Bell Canyon Preservation Trailhead. The trailhead is on the east side of the parking lot (GPS: 40.571405 / -111.797779). Trailhead address: 9971 Wasatch Blvd., Sandy.

Alternatively, reach the trailhead and parking from I-15 south of Salt Lake City. Take exit 295 onto 9000 South/UT 209. Drive east on UT 209, which becomes 9400 South and then Little Cottonwood Road, for 5.9 miles to the junction with Wasatch Boulevard. Go right on Wasatch and drive 0.1 mile south to the left turn, signed "Bell Canyon Preservation Trailhead."

The Hike

Bells Canyon Creek, rising from springs and snowmelt on the north face of 11,253-foot Lone Peak in the central Wasatch Range, dashes down Bells Canyon, a long, glaciated valley. The creek rumbles over a couple small waterfalls in its upper drainage before plunging 80 feet down a granite cliff at "Upper Bells Canyon Falls." A long

June snowmelt brings whitewater tumult and mist to "Lower Bells Canyon Falls,"
one of the most popular waterfalls near Salt Lake City.

Bells Canyon Waterfalls

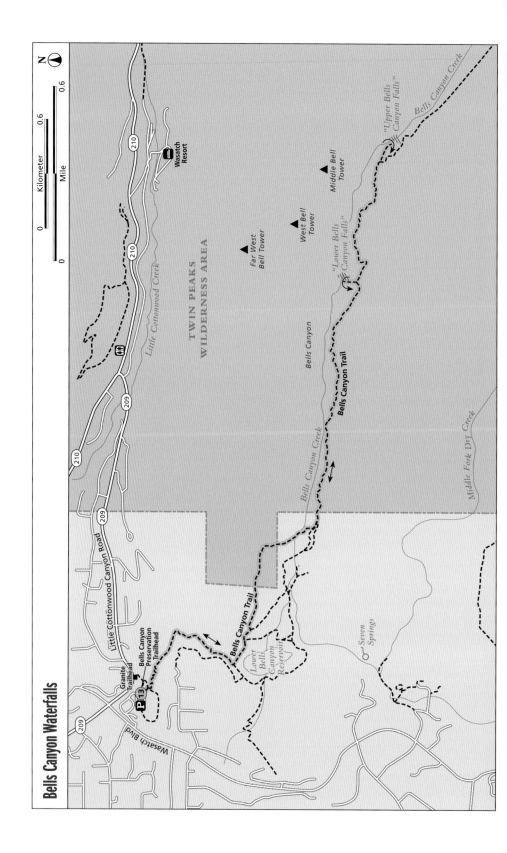

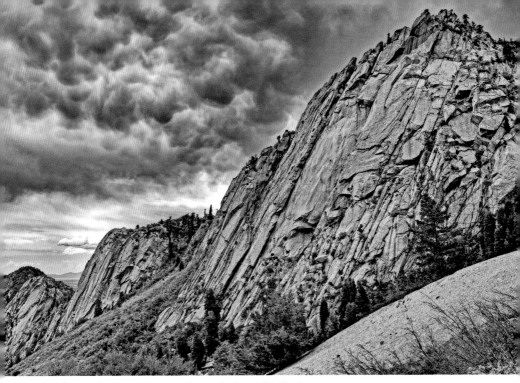

The three Bell Towers dominate the north slope of Bells Canyon.

stretch of cascading whitewater leads to "Lower Bells Canyon Falls," a 65-foot horse-tail waterfall that pours off a granite bench and shatters to mist on boulders below.

Bells Canyon Trail, beginning at a trailhead off Wasatch Boulevard, is a popular hike up the scenic valley to the waterfalls. Most walkers turn around after enjoying the impressive lower falls, but only a few hardy hikers continue another half hour to the upper waterfall. With regularly spaced signposts, the trail is easy to follow to the first waterfall. Bring your route-finding skills to reach the base of the upper falls, since the trail becomes faint and hard to follow in places. Follow the sound of falling water to reach the waterfalls. To see the top of the upper falls, continue up the trail through woods to the right of the falls to a viewpoint on a white granite slab. Parts of Bell Canyon Trail are rough and rocky, so bring trekking poles for balance.

The waterfalls are best in May and June, when runoff from deep snow on Lone Peak fills the waterfalls. Use extreme care at the falls during high-water season. Many accidents and fatalities have occurred here. Later in summer the flow lessens, but the waterfalls are still noisy and gorgeous.

Miles and Directions

0.0 From the trailhead on the east side of the parking lot, go straight on a trail that bends right.

0.03 Reach a junction and go left on Bells Canyon Trail (signs with a blue "A" designate the trail to the first falls). Hike 50 feet up the trail to a junction on the left with Granite Trail, which climbs 0.15 mile from Granite Trailhead on Little Cottonwood Canyon Road. Follow the trail

Lupines cover a Gambel oak–fringed meadow on the Bells Canyon Trail.

uphill, making eight switchbacks. Then continue, steadily gaining elevation, to the north side of Lower Bells Canyon Reservoir.

0.6 Reach a junction at the tree-lined lake and go left on Bells Canyon Trail (GPS: 40.566742 / -111.795783). Hike east on a closed service road.

0.75 Reach a signed junction on the left (GPS: 40.565873 / -111.793481). Go left on the singletrack trail and continue east through Gambel oak thickets and meadows on the valley bottomlands.

1.2 Cross a footbridge over the creek to its south bank (GPS: 40.562665 / -111.786756). Continue east on the stony trail and enter the Lone Peak Wilderness Area. The trail begins climbing here, following the creek's south side and clambering over boulders.

2.2 After crossing a side creek, reach a junction with a short trail to "Lower Bells Canyon Falls" (GPS: 40.560467 / -111.770543). Go left on the rough path to the waterfall.

2.25 Arrive at the base of the lower falls (GPS: 40.561125 / -111.770480). Return to the main trail and go left to hike to the upper falls. The trail climbs to a left turn and levels out in meadows and scattered trees with views of Middle Bell Tower to the north. Begin gently climbing past bedrock slabs to a junction.

2.7 At the junction, look left and follow a less-used trail. Descend across slopes to the creek. Continue to the base of the waterfall. From the junction, the main trail bends right and continues up wooded slopes to the top of the falls. (**Option:** After returning to the main trail, go right to return to the trailhead for a 4.5-mile out-and-back hike.)

2.8 Arrive at the base of "Upper Bells Canyon Falls" (GPS: 40.558777 / -111.761501). Enjoy the thunder of falling water and solitude, then return down the trail.

3.4 Reach the junction with the lower falls trail. Continue down the trail.

5.6 Arrive back at the trailhead (GPS: 40.571405 / -111.797779).

Southern Wasatch Range

Provo, Pleasant Grove, Orem, Sundance Mountain Resort

One of Utah's best waterfalls, "Timpanogos Falls" brings grace and beauty to the Mount Timpanogos Trail.

14 Battle Creek Waterfalls: "Battle Creek Falls," "Middle Battle Creek Falls," "Upper Battle Creek Falls"

"Battle Creek Falls," a popular hiking destination on the edge of Utah Valley, plummets 50 feet off a steep limestone cliff into a cliff-lined canyon.

Start: Battle Creek Trailhead
Trail: Battle Creek Trail (#050)
Difficulty: Moderate
Hiking time: About 1 hour
Distance: 1.2 miles out and back; 1.4 miles out and back to upper falls
Elevation trailhead to falls viewpoint: 5,245 to 5,610 feet (+365 feet)
Trail surface: Dirt and gravel on closed road
Restrictions: Leashed dogs only

Amenities: Vault toilets and picnic tables at Kiwanis Park by the trailhead; services in Pleasant Grove, Orem, and Provo
Maps: *Benchmark Maps:* Page 51 E11; Trails Illustrated #709: Wasatch Front North; USGS Orem
County: Utah
Land status/contact: Uinta-Wasatch-Cache National Forest, Pleasant Grove Ranger District, (801) 785-3563

Finding the trailhead: From exit 275 on I-15 south of Provo in Pleasant Grove, drive northeast on West Pleasant Grove Boulevard for 1.1 miles; turn right on West 220 S Street. Drive east for 3 miles on West 220 S, which becomes West 200 S Street at State Street, to Battle Creek Trailhead, Kiwanis Park, and a large parking lot (GPS: 40.362960 / -111.700565). The signed trailhead is on the north side of the lot.

The Hike

Battle Creek, originating below the summit of iconic 11,755-foot Mount Timpanogos, plunges more than 5,000 feet from its headwaters to "Battle Creek Falls." Tucked into a cliff-lined amphitheater, the waterfall plunges 50 feet off a vertical limestone cliff to a spray of whitewater on rocks below. The falls, hidden in a canyon on the east edge of the Utah Valley metropolis, is reached by a popular hike up Battle Creek Trail, which continues above the main falls to a couple smaller waterfalls, then climbs to Curly Springs and Dry Canyon Trails.

A somber event in March 1849 gave Battle Creek Canyon, the waterfall, and the creek their name. After reports of cow killings and horse rustling by the Timpanogos band of native people in Utah Valley filtered up to Salt Lake City, Mormon leaders sent militiamen to investigate. Even after the horse-theft accusation proved false, the militia surrounded a group of Timpanogos men in Battle Creek Canyon at night. The

"Battle Creek Falls" slip slides over a vertical limestone cliff in a deep canyon. ▶

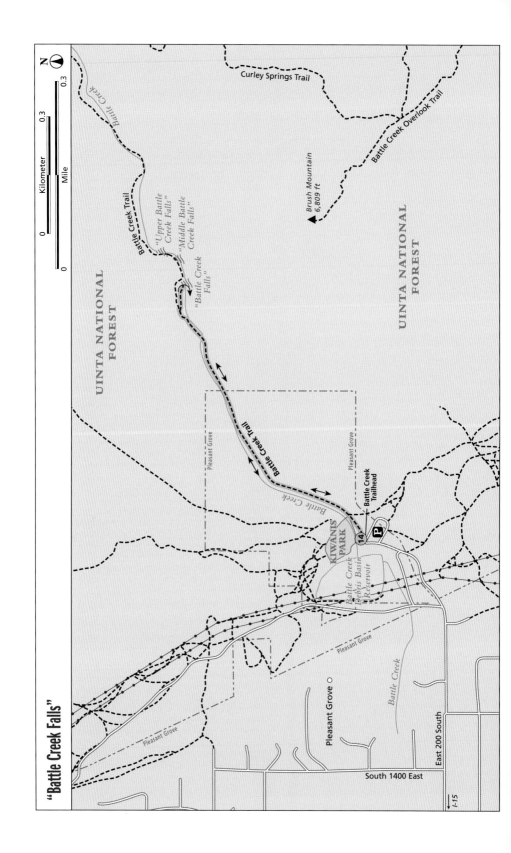

"Battle Creek Falls"

Lovely "Upper Battle Creek Falls" fills two water-carved punchbowls.

men tried to flee after awakening in the morning, and "seven great, fat, stout men" were killed. The skirmish at the canyon's mouth was the first armed engagement between Mormon settlers and Native Americans in the area.

The trail, beginning at wooded Kiwanis Park, follows a closed road up the dry canyon to a grate, where the creek's flow diverts for downstream use. Past here, the trail threads along the creek and then dips down to the waterfall base. Use caution below the waterfall—limestone chunks occasionally fall from the cliff above. The trail continues above the falls to a couple small waterfalls. The falls, reduced to a trickle by midsummer, are best seen in spring and early summer.

Miles and Directions

0.0   Start at the Battle Creek Falls Trailhead and hike northeast on the trail, a wide dirt road, into a deep canyon lined with broken cliffs.

0.3   Reach a diversion dam and pipe. Continue east on the singletrack trail.

0.5   Reach a junction with a side trail on the right. Descend the stony trail to the base of the waterfall.

0.6   Arrive at the base of "Battle Creek Falls" (GPS: 40.367391 / -111.693004). After admiring the falls, return down the trail.

1.2   Arrive back at the trailhead (GPS: 40.362960 / -111.700565).

Extra credit: To see the two small upper waterfalls above Battle Creek Falls, continue up the main trail past the turnoff to the base of the big waterfall. Hike 0.1 mile, passing above the waterfall to "Middle Battle Creek Falls" and the highest waterfall, 12-foot "Upper Battle Creek Falls," which splashes into a bedrock punchbowl (GPS: 40.367761 / -111.692045). Return to the junction for a 0.2-mile diversion. Caution: Take extreme care on the trail above "Battle Creek Falls;" it is unfenced, and a fall would be fatal.

15 Bridal Veil Falls

Two hikes explore Bridal Veil Falls, Utah's highest waterfall, which roars over two limestone cliff bands and a long cascade on the rugged south flank of Provo Canyon, a deep gorge excavated by the Provo River.

Start: Informal trailhead at north side of footbridge
Trails: Provo River Parkway (accessible), Bridal Veil Falls Trail
Difficulty: Easy and moderate
Hiking time: 30 minutes–1 hour
Distance: 0.2 mile out and back to viewpoint by Provo River; 0.5 mile out and back to falls base
Elevation trailhead to falls viewpoint: 5,125 to 5.120 feet (-5 feet); 5,125 to 5,345 feet (+220 feet)
Trail surface: Paved, dirt, rocks
Restrictions: Park closed mid-Oct to early Apr for avalanche safety. Park at gate on the scenic

drive road to hike to overlook by river. Follow the trail to base of waterfall; do not shortcut trail, and do not climb to waterfall base along the lower cascade. Follow Leave No Trace principles.
Amenities: Restrooms, picnic area; wheelchair-accessible trail; highway overlook; services in Orem and Provo
Maps: *Benchmark Maps:* Page 51 C11; Trails Illustrated #709: Wasatch Front North; USGS Bridal Veil Falls
County: Utah
Land status/contact: Utah County Parks and Trails, (801) 851-8640

Finding the trailhead: From I-15 in Provo, take exit 272 and drive east on 800 North/UT 52 for 4.1 miles to Provo Canyon Road/US 189. Drive northeast up the canyon on four-lane Provo Canyon Road for 3.2 miles to a right turn, signed "Bridal Veil Park" and "Upper Falls Park," onto Old Provo Canyon Road/North Provo River Scenic Drive. Follow the road past a parking area on the right used for winter hikers and climbers and pass a gate at a bridge over the Provo River. Pass strip parking on the right, which accesses Bridal Veil Picnic Area, and continue to parking lots on the right. After parking, start the Provo River Parkway hike and the Bridal Veil Falls Trail by walking up the road to an informal trailhead at the footbridge over the Provo River. GPS: 40.341174 / -111.602536

The Hike

Two-tiered Bridal Veil Falls, Utah's tallest and most famous waterfall, plunges over two limestone cliffs and then cascades down a steep, rocky streambed for a 607-foot vertical drop to a viewing area next to the Provo River. The waterfall, one of thirty-nine Bridal Veil Falls in twenty-five states, was named in the 1880s by visitors for its resemblance to the lacy white veil worn by period women on their wedding day. One

Two-tiered Bridal Veil Falls, Utah's highest waterfall, drops 607 feet from the top of its upper falls to the bottom of the cascade at the Provo River. ▶

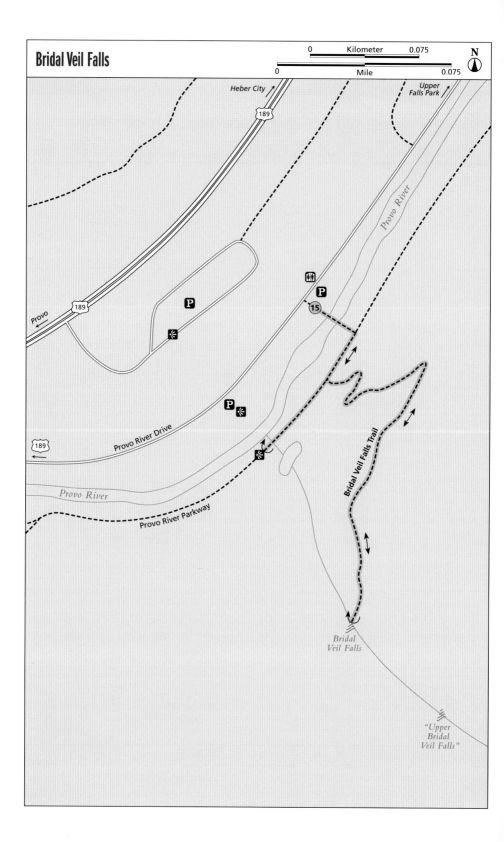

Bridal Veil Falls

Kilometer
0   0.075

Mile
0   0.075

N

Heber City

Upper
Falls Park

189

Provo River

Provo

189

P

P

15

189

Provo River Drive

Bridal Veil Falls Trail

Provo River

Provo River Parkway

Bridal
Veil Falls

"Upper
Bridal
Veil Falls"

of Utah's natural crown jewels, Bridal Veil Falls, the state's most popular waterfall, lies a scant 4 miles from Orem's eastern suburbs in the Wasatch Mountains.

Reach the base of the lower cascade from parking areas on Provo River Scenic Drive on the paved, accessible Provo River Parkway trail, while rugged Bridal Veil Falls Trail steeply climbs loose slopes to broken ledges below the waterfall's spectacular second tier. Both hikes are described in this chapter.

An unnamed creek, fed by springs and snowmelt, on the north slope of 10,908-foot Cascade Mountain keeps Bridal Veil Falls flowing year-round, although spring and early summer offer the best views of falling water. In winter the waterfall freezes into an icy chandelier, attracting ice climbers to its vertical ribs. Extreme avalanche danger closes the falls area to hikers in winter. View the winter wonderland from the highway overlook.

The waterfall, protected in Utah County's Bridal Veil Park, has long been a tourist attraction. Bridal Veil Falls Resort operated at the base for most of the twentieth century. The resort built Eagle's Nest Lodge, with a restaurant, dance hall, and visitor center, in 1967 on a cliff edge high above the upper falls. Visitors traveled to the lodge on an aerial tramway that was at the time the steepest in the world, with an average angle of 45 degrees. Many passengers freaked out with the exposure and steepness of the airy ride. In 1996 an avalanche destroyed the tramway, and in 2008, a fire consumed the abandoned restaurant. The cable and lodge debris were removed from the mountain, returning Bridal Veil Falls to an unadulterated state.

Miles and Directions

Provo River Parkway Hike

0.0 Start at the informal trailhead at the north side of the footbridge over the Provo River. Cross the bridge for 105 feet to Provo River Parkway.

0.02 Reach the paved Provo River Parkway, a wide footpath, and go right.

0.1 Reach a wide bridge and Bridal Veil Falls overlook on the trail beside a pool. Enjoy views of the waterfall and cascade above the trail. Return east on Provo River Parkway to the footbridge.

0.2 Arrive back at the trailhead (GPS: 40.341174 / -111.602536).

Bridal Veil Falls Trail

0.0 Start at the informal trailhead at the north side of the footbridge over the Provo River. Cross the bridge for 105 feet to Provo River Parkway.

0.02 Reach the paved Provo River Parkway and go right for 125 feet.

0.05 Reach a junction on the left for Bridal Veil Falls Trail, signed "Steep Narrow Trail Proceed at Your Own Risk." Go left on the dirt and rock trail. Climb past three switchbacks and then begin steadily climbing up to the right across scree slopes interspersed with clumps of trees. The trail is narrow and exposed in places.

0.25 Arrive at limestone ledges at the base of Bridal Veil Falls (GPS: 40.339318 / -111.602204). Use extreme caution below the falls because of slick and loose rock. After cooling in the waterfall's spray, return down the trail to Provo River Parkway.

0.5 Arrive back at the trailhead (GPS: 40.341174 / -111.602536).

16 Upper Falls

An unnamed creek fed by springs rushes down Davis Canyon to Upper Falls, a four-tier waterfall that drops over limestone cliff bands. Hikers can easily visit the lowest falls, a gorgeous horsetail waterfall in a rock-lined amphitheater.

Start: Upper Falls Trailhead
Trail: Upper Falls Trail
Difficulty: Moderate
Hiking time: About 1 hour
Distance: 0.6 mile out and back
Elevation trailhead to falls viewpoint: 5,160 to 5,515 feet (+355 feet)
Trail surface: Dirt, rocks
Restrictions: Fee area. Day use only from 6 a.m. to 10 p.m.; park closed mid-Oct to early Apr for avalanche safety. No alcoholic beverages; no camping; no fires outside established firepits; fireworks prohibited. Do not shortcut trail. Follow Leave No Trace principles.
Amenities: Restrooms, picnic area; services in Orem and Provo
Maps: *Benchmark Maps:* Page 51 C11; Trails Illustrated #709: Wasatch Front North; USGS Bridal Veil Falls
County: Utah
Land status/contact: Uinta-Wasatch-Cache National Forest, Pleasant Grove Ranger District, (801) 785-3563

Finding the trailhead: From I-15 in Provo, take exit 272 and drive east on 800 North/UT 52 for 4.1 miles to Provo Canyon Road/US 189. Drive northeast up the canyon on four-lane Provo Canyon Road for 3.2 miles to a right turn, signed "Bridal Veil Park" and "Upper Falls Park," onto Old Provo Canyon Road/ Provo River Scenic Drive. Follow the road for 2 miles, passing a gate at a bridge over the Provo River and the footbridge and trailhead for Bridal Veil Falls, to a right turn into the parking lot for Upper Falls Park, labeled "Upper Falls Picnic Area." The trailhead is at the footbridge over the Provo River. GPS: 40.346660 / -111.593827

Alternatively, instead of taking the right turn to Bridal Veil Park, continue northeast on US 189 for 1.5 miles to a sharp right turn onto Provo River Scenic Drive. Drive 0.4 mile to a left turn into Upper Falls Park.

The Hike

Everyone marvels at Bridal Veil Falls, Utah's tallest waterfall, but just up the road from Bridal Veil's busy parking lots and trails hides Upper Falls, a noisy horsetail waterfall that is rarely visited when compared with its big brother. The lowest plunge of the frothy, four-tier waterfall pours almost 50 feet off a limestone cliff in Davis Canyon, the first canyon east of Bridal Veil Falls. A short, steep hike scrambles to the base of the falls, where you can stand in misty spray on steamy afternoons. Bring trekking poles; the footing is slippery on the rocky trail.

Upper Falls is the centerpiece of Upper Falls Park, a national forest recreation area maintained by Utah County Parks. Besides the trail to the waterfall, the site offers picnic tables with firepits, vault toilets, and majestic mountain views. Upper Falls

Upper Falls

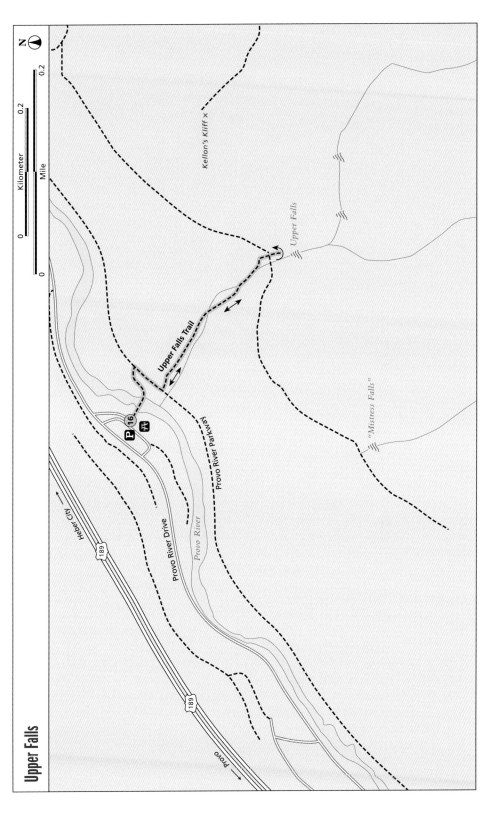

N

Kilometer
0   0.2   0.2
Mile

Kellon's Kliff ×

Upper Falls

Upper Falls Trail

"Mistress Falls"

P 16

Provo River Drive

Provo River

Provo River Parkway

Heber City

189

189

Provo

Upper Falls, east of famed Bridal Veil Falls, pours over limestone cliff bands in Provo Canyon.

Resort, with a café, gas station, dance hall, twenty-two cabins, and icehouse, once spread across the site of today's park on the Provo River.

After visiting the lower falls, intrepid hikers can reach the second tier by hiking left from the lower falls on a trail and then cutting back right on ledges above a cliff to a viewpoint of the second tier of Upper Falls, a twin waterfall that rumbles off a cliff band. Hikers with climbing experience and a rope for safety can scramble to the two highest waterfalls in Davis Canyon. Another waterfall, "Mistress Falls," lies in the next drainage west of Upper Falls. Reach it by following a narrow primitive trail along the cliff base to the waterfall, which sprays off a couple cliff bands. Expect rough hiking, route-finding, and exposure. "Mistress Falls" has less water than Upper Falls.

Miles and Directions

0.0 Start at the unofficial trailhead at the footbridge by the parking lot. Cross the bridge and keep left at a trail junction.

0.06 Turn right on the paved Provo River Parkway, a trail that heads west to Bridal Veil Falls.

0.1 Reach a junction and Upper Falls Trailhead on the left (GPS: 40.346174 / -111.593252) at concrete ruins. Go left on the trail and begin climbing steep, wooded slopes.

0.3 Reach the base of the lowest waterfall of Upper Falls (GPS: 40.344430 / -111.590690). Return down the trail to Provo River Parkway.

0.6 Arrive back at the trailhead (GPS: 40.346660 / -111.593827).

17 Stewarts Cascades

Plunging almost 200 feet off a cliff below Mount Timpanogos, two-tiered Stewarts Cascades is one of Utah's most dramatic waterfalls and a real crowd-pleaser.

Start: Aspen Grove Trailhead
Trail: Stewarts Cascades Trail (#056)
Difficulty: Moderate
Hiking time: About 2 hours
Distance: 3.4 miles out and back
Elevation trailhead to falls viewpoint: 6,892 to 6,882 feet (-10 feet); round-trip elevation gain, 677 feet
Trail surface: Dirt, rocks
Restrictions: Fee area. Wilderness rules apply. Hikers only, group size limited to 15 people; shortcutting switchbacks is prohibited. No fires; pack out garbage; bury human waste. Motorized equipment and mechanized vehicles are prohibited. Follow Leave No Trace principles.
Amenities: Vault toilets and picnic tables at trailhead area; drinking water at trailhead; Mount Timpanogos Campground; services at Sundance Resort
Maps: *Benchmark Maps:* Page 51 C11; Trails Illustrated #709: Wasatch Front North; USGS Aspen Grove
County: Utah
Land status/contact: Uinta-Wasatch-Cache National Forest, Pleasant Grove Ranger District, (801) 785-3563

Finding the trailhead: From Salt Lake City, drive south on I-15 to exit 284 in Lehi. Head east on UT 92 for 7.2 miles to a junction with UT 146 at the mouth of American Fork Canyon. Continue east on UT 92 up the canyon, passing a fee station and Timpanogos Cave National Monument, for 5.1 miles to a junction with UT 146. Keep right on UT 92 (Alpine Loop Scenic Byway) and drive the twisty road for 9.8 miles to Aspen Grove Trailhead on the right. Stewarts Cascades Trailhead is at the southwest corner of the parking lot. GPS: 40.404650 / -111.605291
  From Provo and points south, take I-15 to exit 272 and go east on UT 51 (800 North) to US 189 (Provo Canyon Road). Go left on US 189; follow it northeast for 6.9 miles and turn left onto UT 92 (Alpine Loop Scenic Byway). Follow UT 92 up a canyon and past Sundance Mountain Resort to a left turn to the trailhead and parking lot after 4.8 miles.

The Hike

Winter storms fill Cascade Cirque, a glacier-carved basin on the southeast slope of 11,755-foot Mount Timpanogos, with over 12 feet of champagne powder. As spring's warm temperatures thaw the deep drifts, meltwater rushes down an unnamed creek in a continuous cascade, broken into at least six waterfalls, for almost 700 feet. Stewarts Cascades, the lowest two-tier waterfall, joyfully pours 180 feet off a limestone cliff into a valley above Sundance Mountain Resort.

  The waterfall, officially named Stewarts Cascades on USGS maps, is often called "Stewart Falls." The waterfall was named for Scottish immigrants Andrew Jackson Stewart and his sons, Andrew, Scott, and John, who homesteaded the area in the late

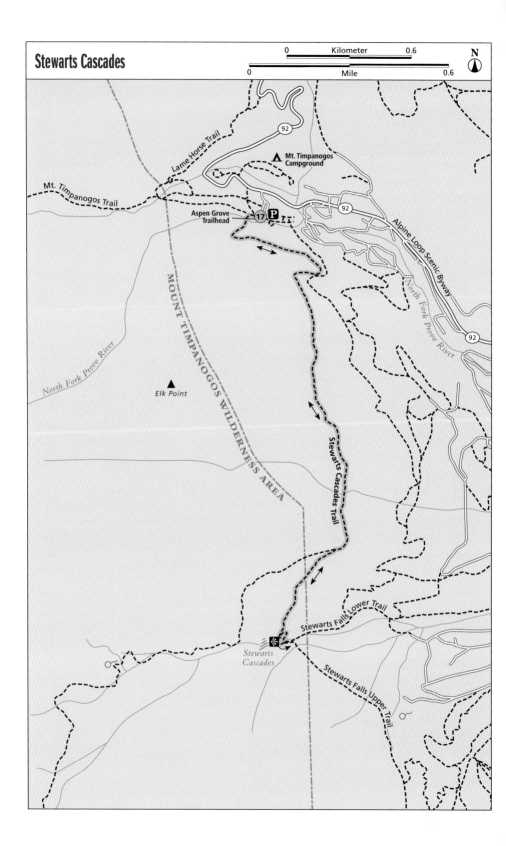

Stewarts Cascades

Kilometer
0   0.6
Mile
0   0.6

N

Lame Horse Trail

92

Mt. Timpanogos
Campground

Mt. Timpanogos Trail

Aspen Grove
Trailhead

17 P

92

Alpine Loop Scenic Byway

North Fork Provo River

North Fork Provo River

92

MOUNT TIMPANOGOS WILDERNESS AREA

Elk Point

Stewarts Cascades Trail

Stewarts Falls Lower Trail

Stewarts
Cascades

Stewarts Falls Upper Trail

Bent by winter avalanches, quaking aspen trees line Stewarts Cascades Trail.

nineteenth century. Actor Robert Redford bought the land in 1969 and founded Sundance Mountain Resort, which he sold in 2020.

Stewarts Cascades Trail, a popular family-friendly hike, threads through tall trees and groves of quaking aspen to a rock-rimmed lookout at the falls. A short trail descends to the foot of the falls and a cooling mist. The trail crosses several avalanche paths, so plan to cross snow and debris in May and June, the best time to view the gushing waterfall. If a snowfield covers the valley below the falls in early summer, do not walk onto the snow—the creek flows beneath the surface, and an unsuspecting hiker could break through the snow, or it could collapse under their weight. Visit the east-facing waterfall in the morning, when sunlight brightens the cliffs and misty water.

Miles and Directions

0.0 Start at the Stewarts Cascades Trailhead, at the southwest corner of the parking lot by the vault toilets. Go up timber steps and walk west to a signed trail junction. Go left toward Stewarts Cascades. Hike south to a switchback, then contour across wooded north-facing slopes.

0.4 Reach a round water tower on the left. The trail heads south, winding through aspen groves, meadows, and across avalanche paths, often snow-covered in June, with bent-over trees.

1.0 Pass over a 7,197-foot high point between avalanche paths and descend through aspen groves to the edge of a broad valley.

1.3 Look through trees for the first view of Stewarts Cascades. For a better glimpse, go 50 feet left on a social trail to the valley rim (GPS: 40.390267 / -111.600849). Continue hiking

Stewarts Cascades, a 180-foot cataract, is a spectacular downpour of snowmelt on the eastern flank of Mount Timpanogos.

southwest across wooded slopes, descending to another avalanche path that holds snow into June. Use caution crossing it.

1.7 Reach a rocky overlook with a spacious view of the plummeting waterfall (GPS: 40.386527 / -111.604306). After enjoying the whitewater, follow the trail back north.

Extra credit: For a view from the bottom of the waterfall, descend a trail from the overlook for 400 feet to the valley below. If snow covers the valley, do not walk onto the snowfield. The creek flows beneath the surface, and a hiker can break through the crust, resulting in severe injury or death.

3.4 Arrive back at the trailhead (GPS: 40.404650 / -111.605291).

18 Timpanogos Waterfalls: "Timpanogos Falls," "Lower Timpanogos Falls"

Fed by snowmelt and springs high on Mount Timpanogos, an unnamed creek twists east from Emerald Lake and Hidden Lakes into steep-sided Primrose Cirque, where it leaps off cliff bands in showy waterfalls.

Start: Aspen Grove Trailhead
Trail: Mount Timpanogos Trail (#052)
Difficulty: Moderate
Hiking time: About 2 hours
Distance: 2.6 miles out and back
Elevation trailhead to falls viewpoint: 6,890 to 7,620 feet (+730 feet)
Trail surface: Dirt, asphalt, rocks
Restrictions: Fee area. Wilderness rules apply; hikers only, group size limited to 15 people; shortcutting switchbacks is prohibited. No fires; pack out garbage; bury human waste. Motorized equipment and mechanized

vehicles are prohibited. Follow Leave No Trace principles.
Amenities: Vault toilets and picnic tables at trailhead area; drinking water at trailhead; Mount Timpanogos Campground; services in Sundance Mountain Resort and Provo
Maps: *Benchmark Maps:* Page 51 C11; Trails Illustrated #709: Wasatch Front North; USGS Aspen Grove
County: Utah
Land status/contact: Uinta-Wasatch-Cache National Forest, Pleasant Grove Ranger District, (801) 785-3563

Finding the trailhead: From Salt Lake City, drive south on I-15 to exit 284 in Lehi. Head east on UT 92 for 7.2 miles to a junction with UT 146 at the mouth of American Fork Canyon. Continue east on UT 92 up the canyon, passing a fee station and Timpanogos Cave National Monument, for 5.1 miles to a junction with UT 146. Keep right on UT 92 (Alpine Loop Scenic Byway) and drive the twisty road for 9.8 miles to Aspen Grove Trailhead on the right. Aspen Grove Trailhead is on the west side of the parking lot. GPS: 40.404650 / -111.605291

From Provo and points south, take I-15 to exit 272 and go east on UT 51 (800 North) to US 189 (Provo Canyon Road). Go left on US 189; follow it northeast for 6.9 miles and turn left onto UT 92 (Alpine Loop Scenic Byway). Follow UT 92 up a canyon and past Sundance Mountain Resort to a left turn, just past a toll booth, to the trailhead and parking lot after 4.8 miles.

The Hike

For a double dose of waterfall glory, take the Mount Timpanogos Trail to enjoy the crash of falling water at two waterfalls: "Lower Timpanogos Falls" and "Timpanogos Falls." Both waterfalls sit beside the popular trail, which climbs 7 miles to the 11,749-foot summit of rugged Mount Timpanogos and one of Utah's most expansive views. The mountain is the centerpiece of the 10,518-acre Mount Timpanogos Wilderness Area.

Timpanogos Waterfalls

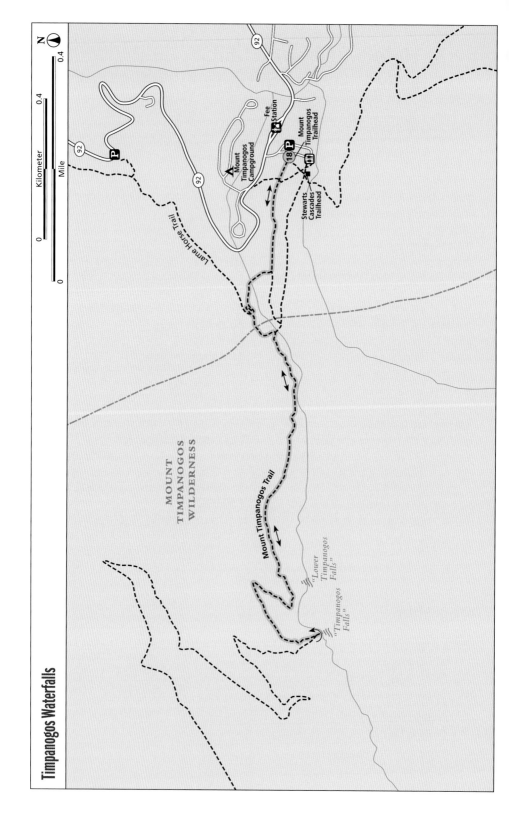

N

Kilometer
0   0.4   0.4

Mile
0   0.4

MOUNT TIMPANOGOS WILDERNESS

92

92

Lame Horse Trail

Mount Timpanogos Campground

Fee Station

18 P

Mount Timpanogos Trailhead

Stewarts Cascades Trailhead

Mount Timpanogos Trail

"Lower Timpanogos Falls"

"Timpanogos Falls"

P

Stray water from "Timpanogos Falls" forms a luxuriant hanging garden of moss and flowers.

"Lower Timpanogos Falls," dropping 60 feet off a cliff, is a two-tiered waterfall. The upper half rumbles over rock benches in a worn groove; the lower section, a horsetail waterfall, spreads a frothy curtain over steep stone. "Timpanogos Falls," another 0.3 mile up the trail, is an impressive 70-foot horsetail waterfall that gushes through a veil of greenery before plummeting off a moss-covered cliff. A verdant hanging garden, fed by a trickling creek, adorns the broken cliff left of the waterfall. While a half dozen more waterfalls—all inaccessible from the trail—lie in the drainage above the second waterfall, two more trailside falls are about 30 minutes farther up the trail.

The Aspen Grove Trailhead and parking lot are popular in summer with Timpanogos hikers, especially on weekends. Come on weekdays to snag a parking spot. The trailhead for the hike to Stewarts Cascades to the south also begins at the parking lot. If you visit the Timpanogos waterfalls early in May or June, do not walk on snowdrifts below the falls. They are hollow, and hikers have fallen through the snow into the hidden creek below. The Mount Timpanogos Trail is renowned for its spectacular wildflower display in late July and early August, with fields of lupine, paintbrush, alpine buttercup, columbine, and elephant head supplying a riot of color.

Miles and Directions

0.0 Start at a trailhead on the west side of the parking lot, signed "Mt. Timpanogos Trail," with a right-pointing arrow. An alternative trailhead is by the restrooms on the far left side of the parking lot. Hike west across a meadow.

0.05 Reach a junction with the alternative trail on the left and the Mount Timpanogos Trailhead. A trailhead sign has area information, including safety, regulations, and weather and a sign for the trail, plus a map and trail info. Water is available here. Continue straight west from the trailhead through forest on the valley floor.

0.2 Reach a closed trail on the left. Keep right on the well-traveled trail and hike through open woods to a bridge over a creek bed (often dry in late summer). Cross a hillside and make two switchbacks through oak groves. The trail enters Mount Timpanogos Wilderness Area at about 0.3 mile.

0.4 Reach a junction with Lame Horse Trail (#055) on the right. Go left and hike west across slopes north of the creek, passing through an oak and aspen woodland. As the trail gently climbs, paved asphalt sections protect the fragile subalpine ecosystem. After 0.6 mile, look west to see the first white waterfall below cliffs.

1.0 Reach a viewpoint at 7,460 feet of "Lower Timpanogos Falls," cascading down a steep chute and then spilling over a cliff (GPS: 40.404547 / -111.620308). A large trailside boulder provides a good look at the waterfall. To see it up close, descend a steep, rocky trail to the base of the falls. Watch for slick, water-polished rock. After viewing the falls, continue up the trail, making a broad contouring switchback across wooded slopes.

1.3 Reach the base of "Timpanogos Falls," pouring down a moss-covered cliff below cliff-rimmed 10,791-foot East Peak (GPS: 40.403857 / -111.621311). A hanging garden spills down a cliff to the left of the waterfall. After enjoying the falls, turn around and return down the trail.

2.6 Arrive back at the trailhead (GPS: 40.404650 / -111.605291).

◀ *"Lower Timpanogos Falls," dropping 60 feet down a stone chute, rages with whitewater fury.*

19 Scout Falls

Scout Falls, filled with snowmelt from Timpanogos Basin below the sheer north face of Mount Timpanogos, rushes off a limestone cliff high in a wooded cirque on the mountain's glaciated northern flank.

Start: Timpooneke Trailhead
Trail: Timpooneke Trail (#053)
Difficulty: Moderate
Hiking time: 2–3 hours
Distance: 3.0 miles out and back
Elevation trailhead to falls viewpoint: 7,365 to 8,190 feet (+825 feet)
Trail surface: Dirt, rocks
Restrictions: Day-use fee payable at trailhead. Wilderness rules apply; hikers only, group size limited to fifteen people; shortcutting switch-backs is prohibited and punishable by fine. No fires; pack out garbage; bury human waste. Motorized equipment and mechanized vehicles are prohibited; follow Leave No Trace principles.
Amenities: Vault toilets and drinking water at trailhead; Timpooneke Campground; services in Sundance Mountain Resort and Provo
Maps: *Benchmark Maps:* Page 51 B11, C11; Trails Illustrated #709: Wasatch Front North; USGS Timpanogos Cave
County: Utah
Land status/contact: Uinta-Wasatch-Cache National Forest, Pleasant Grove Ranger District, (801) 785-3563

Finding the trailhead: From Salt Lake City, drive south on I-15 to exit 284 in Lehi. Head east on UT 92 for 7.2 miles to a junction with UT 146 at the mouth of American Fork Canyon. Continue east on UT 92 up the canyon, passing a fee station and Timpanogos Cave National Monument, for 5.1 miles to a junction with UT 146. Keep right on UT 92 (Alpine Loop Scenic Byway) and drive the twisty road for 8.4 miles to a stop sign. Turn right (west) on FR 056/Timpooneke Road, signed "Timpooneke Campground," and drive 0.3 mile, passing turns into the campground, to a left turn into a large parking lot and Timpooneke Trailhead. GPS: 40.431141 / -111.639166

From Provo and points south, take I-15 to exit 272 and go east on UT 51 (800 North) to US 189 (Provo Canyon Road). Go left on US 189; follow it northeast for 6.9 miles and turn left onto UT 92 (Alpine Loop Scenic Byway). Follow UT 92 up a canyon, passing Sundance Mountain Resort and the turnoff to Aspen Grove Trailhead. Continue on the winding road to a stop sign at a three-way junction and go straight on FR 056/Timpooneke Road toward signed "Timpooneke Campground" (right turn is UT 92). Drive 0.3 mile past turns into the campground to a left turn into a large parking lot and Timpooneke Trailhead.

The Hike

Mount Timpanogos, at 11,755 feet the second-highest peak in the Wasatch Range, towers above Utah Lake and the Provo metro area. The east side of the three-summitted mountain offers a verdant hideaway with mature spruce and fir forests, aspen glades, alpine meadows sprinkled with wildflowers, glacier-carved cirques, and thundering waterfalls.

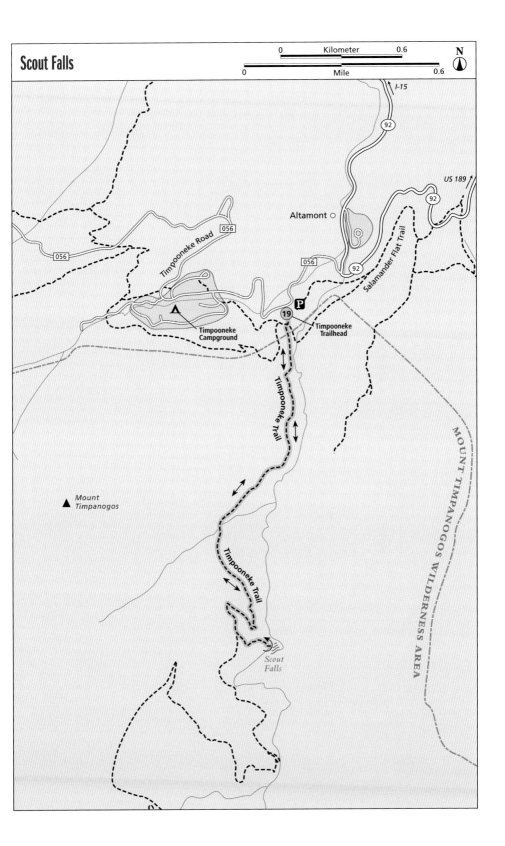

Scout Falls

I-15

92

US 189

92

Altamont ○

056

Timpooneke Road

056

056

92

Salamander Flat Trail

P

19

Timpooneke Trailhead

Timpooneke Campground

Timpooneke Trail

▲ Mount Timpanogos

Timpooneke Trail

Scout Falls

MOUNT TIMPANOGOS WILDERNESS AREA

One of the mountain's best waterfalls is Scout Falls, a glorious twin waterfall that plunges over a vertical limestone cliff through a hanging garden of moss, ferns, and flowers. The horsetail falls, fed by snowmelt and springs in Timpanogos Basin above, is easily reached by Timpooneke Trail, one of two trails that climb to the rocky summit of Mount Timpanogos. The trail to the top twists up three cirques called the Giant Staircase. Scout Falls sprays off the head of the lowest cirque.

The waterfall hike begins at Timpooneke Trailhead off Alpine Scenic Loop Backway, a paved scenic drive that spirals around the north and east flanks of Mount Timpanogos. The easily followed trail threads through a thick woodland interspersed with broad aspen-fringed meadows. Look for grazing elk and moose browsing the wetlands in the valley below the waterfall.

Caution: If you continue hiking past Scout Falls to Timpanogos's summit, be ready for severe weather. Carry sufficient food and drink and have crampons and an ice ax if any snow lingers on the high slopes. Every year the Timpanogos Emergency Response Team rescues unprepared hikers on the mountain.

Miles and Directions

0.0 Begin to the right of vault toilets on the south side of the parking lot. Pay the user fee here, check out maps and wilderness info, then walk south on the trail.

0.02 Reach a three-way trail junction with more information signs and a check station staffed by the Timpanogos Emergency Response Team (TERT) during summer weekends, when the trail is busy with summit hikers. Continue straight on signed Timpooneke Trail. Hike south on slopes west of a creek, passing through aspen, fir, and spruce groves.

0.5 Reach a viewpoint of a broad open valley with the twisting creek flanked by clumps of willow and meadows. Moose often graze in the valley. Hike south on east-facing slopes, gradually gaining elevation. Look straight ahead to see the waterfall pouring off a cliff at the head of the valley.

1.1 Reach a switchback with a view left of Scout Falls. Continue up the trail, climbing right to a wide switchback and then back left.

1.4 Reach a sharp switchback above a steep rocky slope (GPS: 40.417176 / -111.640863). Go left on an unmarked trail. Climb up and over exposed tree roots to a better trail that edges shelflike above broken cliff bands and then contours below a cliff.

1.5 Arrive at the base of Scout Falls (GPS: 40.416962 / -111.640299). Admire the waterfall and then return to the main trail.

1.6 Reach Timpooneke Trail at the switchback. Go right and descend the trail. Look across the valley as you hike down to see an unnamed waterfall rumbling off a cliff band.

3.0 Arrive back at the trailhead (GPS: 40.431141 / -111.639166).

Elegant Scout Falls drops off a cliff band below Timpanogos Basin in the Wasatch Range.

20 Fifth Water Creek Waterfalls: "Lower Fifth Water Creek Falls," "Middle Fifth Water Creek Falls," "Upper Fifth Water Creek Falls"

Fifth Water Trail follows its namesake creek up a wooded valley to popular Fifth Water Hot Springs and three waterfalls—cascading "Lower Fifth Water Creek Falls," single-drop sheet "Middle Fifth Water Creek Falls," and two-tiered horsetail "Upper Fifth Water Creek Falls"—in low mountains east of Spanish Fork.

Start: Three Forks Trailhead
Trail: Fifth Water Trail (#015)
Difficulty: Moderate
Hiking time: 2–3 hours
Distance: 4.8 miles out and back
Elevation trailhead to upper falls viewpoint: 5,550 feet to 6,270 feet (+720 feet)
Trail surface: Dirt, rocks
Restrictions: Parking is limited at the trailhead; do not park on entrance road to trailhead; no roadside parking on Diamond Fork Road except in designated and numbered pullouts; all tires must be entirely off the road. No trailers or camping allowed at the trailhead parking lot. No garbage service at trailhead; pack out all trash. No water at trailhead. Dogs must be leashed in busy trail areas; pick up and pack out all dog waste to protect the watershed. Bury human waste or use a WAG bag, RESTOP, or other portable toilet kit. Horses and mountain bikes share the trail. Health advisory: There are cyanobacteria in the hot springs.
Amenities: Toilets and trail map at trailhead; campgrounds nearby; services in Spanish Fork
Maps: *Benchmark Maps:* Page 52 F2–3; Trails Illustrated #701: Wasatch Front South; USGS Rays Valley
County: Utah
Land status/contact: Uinta-Wasatch-Cache National Forest, Salt Lake Ranger District, (801) 733-2660

Finding the trailhead: From I-15 in Spanish Fork, take exit 257 onto US 6/89 and drive east through Spanish Fork Valley for 10.6 miles to a left turn (signed "Diamond C.G.") onto Diamond Fork Road/CR 029 just past milepost 184. Drive north on paved Diamond Fork Road for 9.8 miles and turn right into the Three Forks Trailhead parking lot. The trailhead is on the lot's east side next to a vault toilet. GPS: 40.084284 / -111.354878

The Hike

Beginning on high ridges in the corrugated foothills east of the Wasatch Range, Fifth Water Creek dances down a deep canyon to a magical haven of hot spring pools and waterfalls. The creek offers two major waterfalls—"Middle Fifth Water Creek Falls"

"Middle Fifth Water Creek Falls" crashes over a cliff
above its famed natural hot springs.

Fifth Water Creek Waterfalls

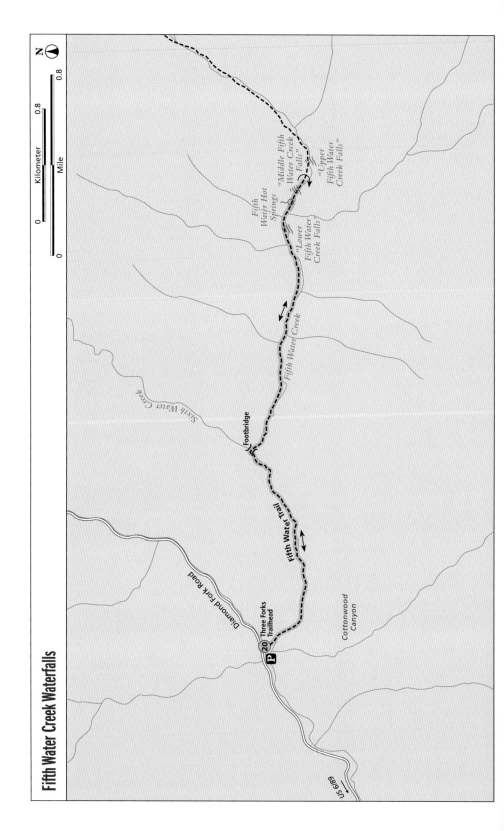

Two-tiered "Upper Fifth Water Creek Falls" offers solitude and beauty to hikers who walk beyond the hot springs.

and "Upper Fifth Water Creek Falls"—along with a long cascade forming "Lower Fifth Water Creek Falls." West of those waterfalls, more small falls are scattered alongside Fifth Water Trail. The main attraction for most hikers is Fifth Water Hot Springs, several human-made soaking pools filled with sulfur-smelling hot water bubbling up from the creek bed. The 12-foot-high middle falls, a sheet waterfall, plunges off a rock ledge and naturally cools the pockets of steamy water. As you hike toward the hot springs, occasional whiffs of sulfur let you know you are near the waterfalls.

The trail, climbing the canyon from Three Forks Trailhead, first reaches the lower cascading waterfall and then a series of hot spring pools tucked against the north bank below the middle falls. These pools form a popular destination for hikers from the Salt Lake City–Provo metroplex, so plan on company, especially on weekends and holidays. Above the middle falls lie a couple of aqua pools with hotter water than the lower ones; farther east hides the third waterfall, 50-foot-high "Upper Fifth Water Creek Falls." Harder to reach than the lower waterfalls, the two-tier cataract plunges over double cliff bands. The best view of the falls looks down from the trail into the rock-walled hollow.

The waterfall and hot spring area receives human use and abuse. Follow existing social trails to the pools and be considerate of other hikers and soakers. Practice a Leave No Trace ethic and pack out your trash as well as litter left behind by less-conscious users. Remember that the hot spring water is dehydrating, so drink plenty of water. Also, since the site is family-friendly, soakers wear bathing suits.

Before soaking in the hot springs, be advised that tests by the Utah Health Department confirm that toxigenic cyanobacteria inhabit the water. Soakers should not submerge their heads or drink water from the hot springs. Keep dogs out of the water, and take a shower as soon as possible after your soak. Avoid body contact with algal mats, where the bacteria live on the bottom of pools. The bright green mats are attached to a rock surface or float in the water. Cyanobacteria produce toxins that cause irritation to the skin, eyes, nose, throat, and lungs. Infected soakers here complain of "swimmer's itch" to their legs, back, and crotch.

Miles and Directions

0.0 Start at the trailhead by a vault toilet and fence. Hike east on the well-trodden trail through woods along Fifth Water Creek and across hillsides high above the creek. Look for rushing cascades and small waterfalls.

1.0 Reach a footbridge over Sixth Water Creek (GPS: 40.085445 / -111.338802) just upstream of its confluence with Fifth Water Creek. Continue east alongside Fifth Water Creek, passing noisy waterfalls pouring over boulders. Before reaching the hot springs, look right for "Lower Fifth Water Creek Falls," a long tumbling cascade.

2.2 Walk past the first hot spring pools by the edge of the creek. Take one of the social trails by the pools to reach the base of "Middle Fifth Water Falls" (GPS: 40.082699 / -111.317949). Return to the main trail on the slope above the falls and hot springs by either climbing a steep trail up left from the top of the waterfall or returning down to the hot springs pools. Continue east up the main trail.

2.4 Reach a viewpoint of gorgeous "Upper Fifth Water Creek Falls" pouring off a cliff (GPS: 40.082129 / -111.316142). The overlook is the turnaround point for the hike. Return west down the trail. (**Option:** It is difficult to reach the base of the falls. From the soaking pools above "Middle Fifth Water Creek Falls," hike up a rough trail alongside the creek, scrambling up eroded slopes and bushwhacking.)

4.8 Arrive back at the trailhead (GPS: 40.084284 / -111.354878).

Central Utah

Payson, Nephi, Manti, Price

Spring runoff fills "Upper Gordon Creek Falls" in a remote canyon west of Price.

21 "Grotto Falls"

A family-friendly hike follows Peteetneet Creek to "Grotto Falls," a noisy waterfall free-falling into The Grotto, a narrow gorge walled with overhanging cliffs.

Start: Grotto Falls Trailhead
Trail: Grotto Trail (#086)
Difficulty: Easy
Hiking time: About 1 hour
Distance: 0.6 mile out and back
Elevation trailhead to falls: 6,390 to 6,530 feet (+140 feet)
Restrictions: Follow existing trails. Pack out trash; dispose of human waste properly. Follow Leave No Trace principles.

Amenities: None at the trailhead; services in Payson
Maps: *Benchmark Maps:* Page 51 G10; Trails Illustrated #701: Wasatch Front South; USGS Payson Lakes
County: Utah
Land status/contact: Uinta-Wasatch-Cache National Forest, Spanish Fork Ranger District, (801) 798-3571

Finding the trailhead: From I-15, take exit 250 to Payson. Drive south on Main Street/UT 115 for 0.7 mile to 100 North and turn left. Drive east on East 100 North for 0.5 mile and turn right on 600 East, following signs for Mount Nebo Scenic Byway. Drive south on 600 East, which becomes Mount Nebo Scenic Byway, for 8.1 miles to a parking lot on the left on a road bend and Grotto Falls Trailhead. GPS: 39.951522 / -111.675642

The Hike

Fed by Peteetneet Creek, popular "Grotto Falls" hides in The Grotto, a secluded canyon off the Mount Nebo Scenic Byway. The 20-foot plunge waterfall, pouring into a stony pool, tucks into a narrow gorge lined with overhanging cliffs south of Payson. Families and kids enjoy the short hike up Grotto Trail but love romping in the cool pool below the falls.

Mountain snowmelt fills the falls in springtime, but the flow ebbs to a trickle by late summer. Winter brings muffled quiet and deep snow to the waterfall, which you reach by hiking an additional 1.5 miles up the road from the winter gate. The Pole Creek Fire burned the area in 2018, leaving standing dead trees above the trail.

One of Utah's most popular waterfalls, "Grotto Falls" ▶
plunges into a cul-de-sac canyon.

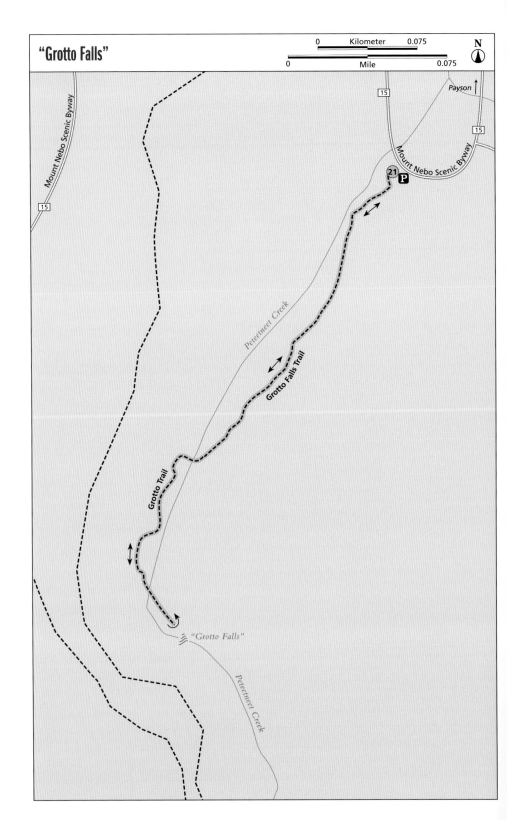

"Grotto Falls"

0   Kilometer   0.075
0   Mile   0.075

N

Payson

15

15

Mount Nebo Scenic Byway

Mount Nebo Scenic Byway

15

21 P

Peteetneet Creek

Grotto Falls Trail

Grotto Trail

"Grotto Falls"

Peteetneet Creek

"Grotto Falls" pours over a notch into a hidden cliff-lined grotto on the Mount Nebo Scenic Byway.

Miles and Directions

0.0   Start at the trailhead on the Mount Nebo Scenic Byway. Hike up the trail along Peteetneet Creek, with occasional creek crossings on logs and passing through a burned area with dead snag trees.

0.3   Reach The Grotto, a cliff-lined cul-de-sac with the waterfall pouring into it. Enjoy the cooling spray and return down the trail.

0.6   Arrive back at the trailhead (GPS: 39.951522 / -111.675642).

22 "Double Falls"

Hidden on an unnamed creek off the Mount Nemo Scenic Byway, two-tiered "Double Falls" rumbles off a vertical cliff to a ledge and then sprays down to a streambed choked with logs and boulders.

Start: Double Falls Trailhead
Trail: Double Falls Trail
Difficulty: Easy
Hiking time: About 1 hour
Distance: 0.7 mile out and back
Elevation trailhead to top of falls: 7,495 to 7,350 feet (-145 feet)
Restrictions: Follow existing trail. Pack out trash and dispose of human waste properly. Follow Leave No Trace principles.

Amenities: None at trailhead; services in Payson
Maps: *Benchmark Maps:* Page 51 H11; Trails Illustrated #701: Wasatch Front South; USGS Payson Lakes
County: Utah
Land status/contact: Uinta-Wasatch-Cache National Forest, Spanish Fork Ranger District, (801) 798-3571

Finding the trailhead: From I-15, take exit 250 to Payson. Drive south on Main Street/UT 115 for 0.7 mile to 100 North and turn left. Drive east on East 100 North for 0.5 mile and turn right on 600 East, following signs for the Mount Nebo Scenic Byway. Drive south on 600 East, which becomes Mount Nebo Scenic Byway, for 11.3 miles to a parking lot on the left side of the road off FR 763 for Jones Ranch Trail. "Double Falls Trailhead" (GPS: 39.942863 / -111.656530), an informal and unmarked trailhead, is to the right of the road and parking lot. Follow a spur road from the parking lot to an open area used as a primitive campsite. Take the unmarked trail heading into aspens.

The Hike

An easy trail passes through aspen groves, pocket meadows, and tall pines to "Double Falls," a dashing two-tiered horsetail waterfall with a double stream pouring off the top. Fed by an unnamed creek, the 40-foot waterfall drops into a shallow canyon just above its confluence with Wimmer Ranch Creek. The waterfall, 3 miles from popular "Grotto Falls," offers a secluded getaway with few hikers.

Use your route-finding skills to locate the waterfall, since the trailhead and trail are unmarked. The singletrack trail is easy to follow as it gently loses elevation. The sound of falling water filters up the trail before your reach the top of "Double Falls." Use caution above the falls—the rock may be wet above a vertical cliff. To reach the base, backtrack from the waterfall's top to a fork and follow a rough trail on the left

The upper tier of "Double Falls" spreads a horsetail spray onto a bedrock ledge.

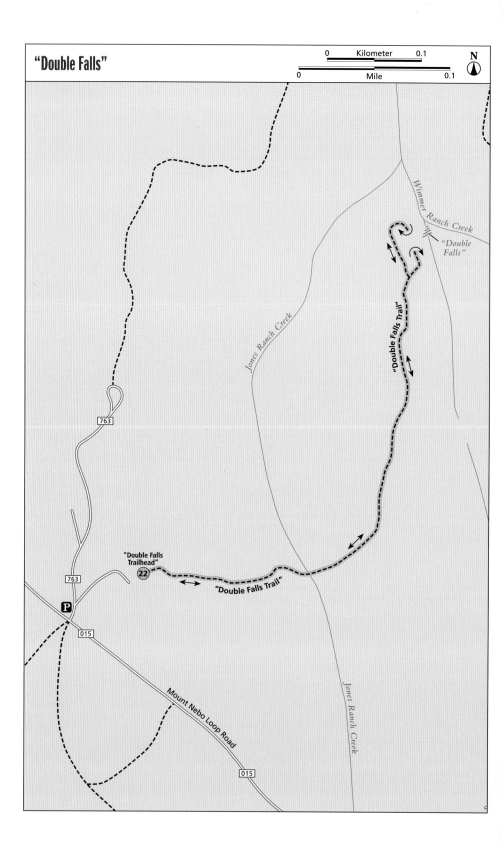

"Double Falls"

0   Kilometer   0.1

0   Mile   0.1

N

Wimmer Ranch Creek

"Double Falls"

"Double Falls Trail"

Jones Ranch Creek

763

"Double Falls Trailhead"

22

"Double Falls Trail"

763

P

015

Mount Nebo Loop Road

015

Jones Ranch Creek

Beginning on Mount Nebo Scenic Byway, the unnamed trail to "Double Falls" passes through meadows and aspen groves.

side of the waterfall and gorge. The last section descends steeply over boulders, tree roots, and compacted soil. A rope for balance is often in place here.

Miles and Directions

0.0 Start at the unmarked trailhead on a spur road northeast of FR 763. Hike east through an aspen forest on the singletrack trail, dipping across Jones Ranch Creek and then bending left and hiking north.

0.35 Reach the top of "Double Falls" (GPS: 39.945871 / -111.653137). To see the waterfall from the base, go left and hike down a steep trail for 260 feet. Afterward, return to the waterfall's top and follow the trail south.

0.7 Arrive back at the trailhead (GPS: 39.942863 / -111.656530).

23 "Salt Creek Falls"

On the eastern slope of Mount Nebo, the southernmost peak in the Wasatch Range, two-tiered "Salt Creek Falls" pours down a frothy cascade to a 12-foot plunge off a cliff.

Start: Salt Creek Trailhead
Trail: Salt Creek Trail (#110)
Difficulty: Moderate
Hiking time: About 2 hours
Distance: 2.7 miles out and back
Elevation trailhead to falls viewpoint: 6,650 to 7,085 feet (+435 feet)
Restrictions: Wilderness regulations apply. Follow existing trails; pack out trash; dispose of human waste properly or use a WAG bag,

RESTOP, or other portable toilet kit. Follow Leave No Trace principles.
Amenities: Toilets and water at Bear Canyon Campground; services in Nephi
Maps: *Benchmark Maps:* Page 59 A10; Trails Illustrated #701: Wasatch Front South; USGS Nebo Basin
County: Juab
Land status/contact: Uinta-Wasatch-Cache National Forest, Spanish Fork Ranger District, (801) 798-3571

Finding the trailhead: From I-15 at Nephi, take exit 225 and drive east on UT 132. After 4.8 miles turn left (north) on paved FR 015, signed "Mt. Nebo National Scenic Byway," and drive north for 3.3 miles to a Y junction. Keep left on Salt Creek Canyon Road/FR 048. The right-hand road is Mount Nebo Scenic Byway. Go north on paved FR 048 for 2.1 miles to the entrance to Bear Canyon Campground. Park in a hiker lot on the right (GPS: 39.786989 / -111.729801). Do not park in the campground. Walk up the campground road to Salt Creek Trailhead on its north side. GPS: 39.788229 / -111.731618

The Hike

Mount Nebo, the 11,941-foot high point of the Wasatch Range and an ultra-prominent peak, towers more than 6,000 feet above Juab Valley on the west and Nemo Basin, a deep valley floored by Salt Creek, on the east. Deep snow blankets Mount Nebo in winter, filling creeks with meltwater that crashes down steep canyons, pouring over waterfalls and forming mile-long whitewater cascades.

The most accessible waterfall is 30-foot "Salt Creek Falls," lying just west of Salt Creek Trail. The scenic trail threads through evergreen forests and aspen groves along the creek to the popular waterfall. The falls is the lowest waterfall on the unnamed creek that drains Middle Basin on Mount Nebo's east flank. The creek boasts at least ten distinct waterfalls, including a couple 85-foot waterfalls that plunge over cliffs,

Beginning high on Mount Nebo, a snowmelt-filled creek
dashes down "Salt Creek Falls."

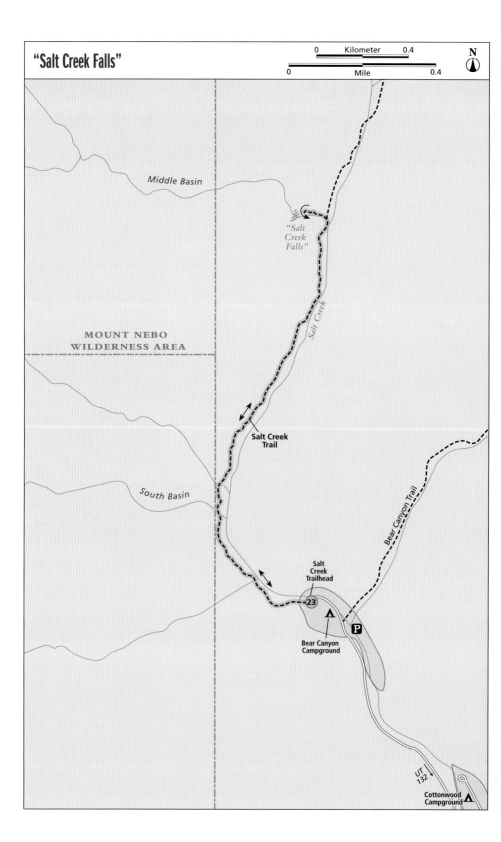

"Salt Creek Falls"

0   Kilometer   0.4

0   Mile   0.4

N

Middle Basin

"Salt Creek Falls"

Salt Creek

MOUNT NEBO
WILDERNESS AREA

Salt Creek Trail

South Basin

Bear Canyon Trail

Salt Creek Trailhead

23

P

Bear Canyon Campground

UT 132

Cottonwood Campground

A fragile snow bridge spans avalanche debris below "Salt Creek Falls."

and continuous cascades. These waterfalls are inaccessible due to steep terrain and cliff bands.

"Salt Creek Falls" is best in late May and June, although it might be inaccessible that early, as it was in 2023, when debris and snow from massive avalanches blocked the trail and covered the waterfall.

Miles and Directions

0.0 Start at the trailhead on the north side of Bear Canyon Campground. Hike north on the trail on slopes above Salt Creek.

1.25 After crossing a side creek, go left on a well-used trail informally called "Salt Creek Falls Trail" (GPS: 39.802520 / -111.730887). Hike up the hillside to the right of the creek.

1.3 Reach the base of "Salt Creek Falls" (GPS: 39.802815 / -111.731990) at 7,080 feet. Return down the trail.

1.35 Reach the junction and go right on Salt Creek Trail.

2.7 Arrive back at the trailhead (GPS: 39.788229 / -111.731618).

24 "Milky Falls"

"Milky Falls," lying east of Manti below the crest of the Wasatch Plateau, is a gorgeous cascade that tumbles and rushes over broken boulders flanked by tall spruce and fir trees.

Start: Informal trailhead on FR 0045
Trail: Unnamed trail
Difficulty: Easy
Hiking time: About 20 minutes
Distance: 0.2 mile out and back
Elevation trailhead to falls viewpoint: 8,345 to 8,370 feet (+25 feet)
Trail surface: Dirt
Restrictions: No motorized vehicles past barrier

Amenities: None; restrooms at Yearns Reservoir on FR 0045; services in Manti
Maps: Benchmark Maps: Page 59 G12; Trails Illustrated #707: Fish Lake, Manti; USGS Black Mountain
County: Sanpete
Land status/contact: Manti-La Sal National Forest, Sanpete Ranger District, (435) 636-3300

Finding the trailhead: Take US 89 to Manti. Turn east on 5th South Street (E 500 S Street), signed for Manti-La Sal National Forest. Drive east on the paved road and leave Manti. After 0.9 mile the road becomes East Manti Canyon Road/FR 0045. Follow the dirt road up deep Manti Canyon past Manti Community Campground to a Y junction at 6.5 miles. Keep right on FR 0045 and follow the narrow road to a parking area on the right at 8.1 miles. The informal trailhead is 100 feet up the road on the left. GPS: 39.243488 / -111.523544

The Hike

Fed by the South Fork of Manti Canyon Creek, which originates at 10,490 feet atop the Wasatch Plateau, "Milky Falls" rages 140 feet down a rock-filled chute in a frothy whitewater cascade. The falls, also fed by Milk Creek, is an easy family-friendly waterfall hike reached by an ATV track and short trail. A bench at an overlook near the waterfall's base is a perfect spot to enjoy the roar of falling water. A rough trail, often muddy, scrambles up steep slopes to the right of the falls for a higher view.

The best views of "Milky Falls" are in late May and June, when snowmelt swells the creek. The waterflow lessens later in the summer. The falls, reached by a narrow USFS road, are accessible from May, after the road is free of snow, until late October. Dispersed campsites lie along the access road near the trailhead and at Bub Arthurs Flat, a grassy meadow before the trailhead. Near Yearns Reservoir is USFS Manti Community Campground.

A short hike reaches "Milky Falls," on the western slope of the Wasatch Plateau. ▶

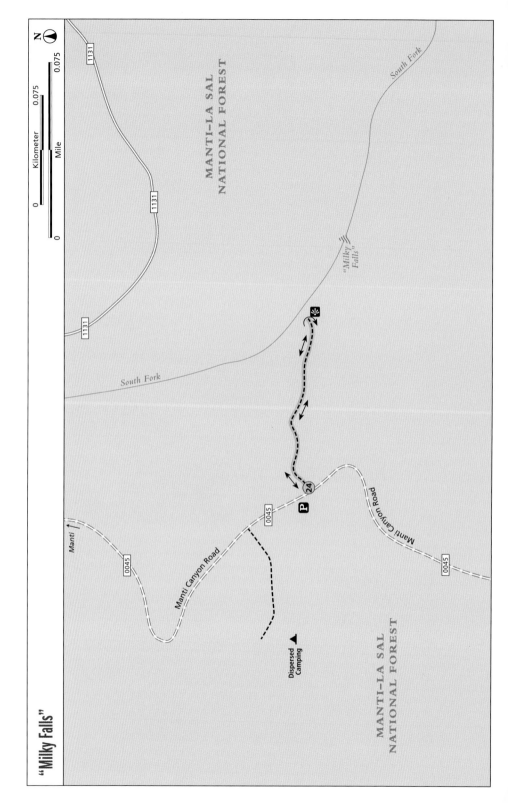

"Milky Falls"

Miles and Directions

0.0 Begin at the trailhead on the east side of the road. Descend a rough track used by ATVs to an aspen grove. Go right past a vehicle barrier and hike up a short trail to the waterfall.

0.1 Arrive at a bench and overlook at the base of "Milky Falls" (GPS: 39.243486 / -111.522222). Enjoy the cascading waterfall and then return to FR 0045.

0.2 Arrive back at the trailhead (GPS: 39.243488 / -111.523544).

25 Gordon Creek Waterfalls: "Gordon Creek Falls," "Upper Gordon Creek Falls"

The South Fork of Gordon Creek offers two waterfalls, reached by a track open to hikers, mountain bikes, and ATVs. The falls drop over sandstone benches in a deep canyon lined with high mesas, broken cliff bands, and a piñon pine and juniper forest.

Start: Gordon Creek Trailhead
Trail: Gordon Creek Trail
Difficulty: Moderate
Hiking time: 1–3 hours
Distance: 5.2 miles out and back to second falls
Elevation trailhead to falls viewpoint: 5,115 to 5,390 feet (+275 feet)
Trail surface: Dirt, sand, rocks

Restrictions: Multiuse trail. ATVs allowed only on the trail past the first waterfall; trail closed to vehicles Dec 1 to Apr 15. Flash flood area— pay attention to weather. Dogs allowed.
Amenities: None; services in Price
Maps: *Benchmark Maps:* Page 60 C6; Trails Illustrated (none); USGS Pinnacle Peak
County: Carbon
Land status/contact: Bureau of Land Management, Price Field Office, (435) 636-3600

Finding the trailhead: From Helper, drive south from exit 232 on US 191 for 2.8 miles or north from exit 240 for Westwood Boulevard in Price on US 191 for 4.5 miles to signed Consumers Road, on the highway's west side. Turn west onto paved Consumers Road and drive west for 2.8 miles to a left turn on unmarked Trestle Road, a dirt road heading southwest just before a large coal mining operation. Follow Trestle Road for 3.4 miles (6.2 miles from US 191) to signed Gordon Creek Trailhead on the right (GPS: 39.621376 / -110.954037). The road is usually passable in a passenger car but requires a high-clearance, four-wheel-drive vehicle in muddy conditions after rain or snow.

The Hike

The South Fork of Gordon Creek, originating from snowmelt on 9,800-foot Castle Valley Ridge atop the broad Wasatch Plateau, twists northeast through a series of canyons lined with cliffs and dry woodlands before dashing over two waterfalls: "Upper Gordon Creek Falls" and "Gordon Creek Falls." Two-tiered, 85-foot "Gordon Creek Falls," the most visited waterfall, tumbles off a bench and then slides down a steep slab to a wide plunge pool in a narrow canyon. The 25-foot upper falls, another 1.5 miles up the canyon, noisily rambles over rock ledges into a shallow inner canyon. Both waterfalls pour over Garley Canyon Sandstone, an erosion-resistant member of the Mancos Shale Formation.

The South Fork of Gordon Creek splashes down a sandstone slab to a murky pool at "Gordon Creek Falls."

Clay cliffs and sandstone mesas surround "Gordon Creek Falls" near Price.

The trailhead, a half dozen miles west of US 191 between Price and Helper, is accessible in a passenger car except after heavy rain or snow, when dirt Trestle Road turns into wheel-binding gumbo. Reach the waterfalls by hiking along a rough four-wheel-drive track and an ATV trail from Trestle Road. While the roads, called Gordon Creek Trail, are open to vehicles from April 16 to November 30, it is just as fast to hike the trails as drive, since both roads have extremely rocky and sandy sections.

Use caution at the viewpoint opposite "Gordon Creek Falls"—it is above soft shale cliffs that regularly collapse. It is also difficult to reach the bottom of the waterfall. To see "Upper Gordon Creek Falls," take a short steep trail down to the falls' base.

Miles and Directions

0.0 Start at the trailhead on the west side of the parking lot and hike northwest on a 4×4 road. Contour across slopes above a canyon and then descend the steep dirt track to the canyon floor.

0.3 Cross the North Fork of Gordon Creek and follow the trail up a steep, rocky section on the canyon's west side. Reach a bench and follow the rough road west. Descend rocky steps and bend left on a flat.

1.05 Reach a junction and go left. Follow an old road near the rim of a deep canyon to a viewpoint.

Gordon Creek Waterfalls

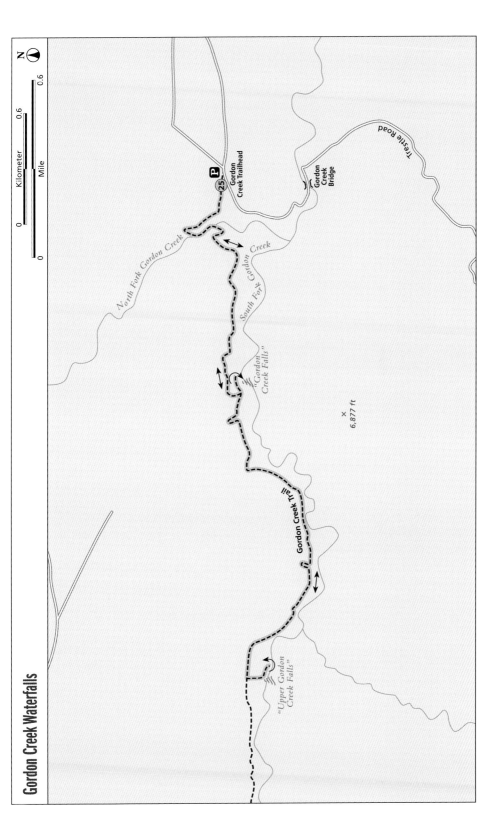

North Fork Gordon Creek

South Fork Gordon Creek

Gordon Creek Trailhead

P

25

Gordon Creek Bridge

Trestle Road

"Gordon Creek Falls"

×
6,877 ft

Gordon Creek Trail

"Upper Gordon Creek Falls"

N

Kilometer
0   0.6   0.6

Mile
0   0.6

"Upper Gordon Creek Falls" tumbles down sandstone steps in a shallow canyon.

1.1 Arrive at an overlook of "Gordon Creek Falls" (GPS: 39.620811 / -110.966038). Be cautious at the canyon's rim; the soft edge could crumble beneath your feet. After viewing the falls, return west on the track.

1.15 Reach the junction and continue straight on a narrow track, open to ATVs. Follow the track west and northwest on a bench north of Gordon Creek.

2.3 Climb a slight rise to the first view of the second waterfall. Continue along the trail across a sagebrush-covered bench and pass a sign marking the boundary of Gordon Creek Wildlife Management Area.

2.5 Reach a junction with an unmarked trail on the left (GPS: 39.620282 / -110.984932). Go left on the trail and follow it west across the flat to a steep descent into the shallow canyon.

2.6 Arrive at the base of "Upper Gordon Creek Falls" (GPS: 39.619165 / -110.984224). Return on the trail to the first waterfall.

4.1 Reach the junction before the first falls. Go left on the trail, climb rocky shelves, and follow the trail east to the North Fork of Gordon Creek and up the steep track on its east slope.

5.2 Arrive back at the trailhead (GPS: 39.621376 / -110.954037).

Northeast Utah

Kamas, Vernal

Seen far below the highway, the Provo River roars over "Upper Slate Gorge Waterfall," a cataract reached only in low water.

26 Provo River Falls: "Upper Provo River Falls," "Middle Provo River Falls," "Lower Provo River Falls," "Upper Slate Gorge Falls"

The Provo River Falls, three waterfalls crashing over striated bedrock ledges, lie alongside Mirror Lake Scenic Byway on the southwest edge of the High Uintas Wilderness Area.

Start: Provo River Falls Trailhead (unofficial name)
Trail: Provo River Falls Trail (unofficial name)
Difficulty: Easy
Hiking time: 30 minutes–1 hour
Distance: 0.2-mile loop
Elevation trailhead to falls viewpoint: 9,345 to 9,335 (upper overlook); 9,300 (middle overlook); 9,285 feet (lower overlook) (-60 feet)
Trail surface: Paved, dirt, rock

Restrictions: UT 150/Mirror Lake Highway closes in winter; highway is usually open Memorial Day to late Oct. Strong river currents.
Amenities: Vault toilets; services in Kamas
Maps: *Benchmark Maps:* Page 44 H6; Trails Illustrated #711: High Uintas Wilderness (Ashley and Uinta-Wasatch-Cache National Forests); USGS Mirror Lake
County: Duchesne
Land status/contact: Uinta-Wasatch-Cache National Forest, Heber-Kamas Ranger District, (435) 783-4338

Finding the trailhead: From the junction of Center and Main Streets in Kamas, drive east on UT 150/Mirror Lake Highway for about 23.5 miles to a left turn into a parking lot, signed "Wasatch National Forest Overlook, Provo River Falls," before milepost 24. Drive 125 feet to a parking lot, restrooms, and the trailhead. GPS: 40.657484 / -110.945883

The Hike

The Provo River, flowing 71 miles from the Unita Mountains to Utah Lake, dashes down a wooded canyon below its headwaters on 11,263-foot Notch Mountain to three cascading waterfalls collectively called Provo River Falls. "Upper Provo River Falls," "Middle Provo River Falls," and "Lower Provo River Falls," lying a few hundred feet off Mirror Lake Scenic Byway, are easily viewed from an easy trail that leads to several overlooks. A mature fir and spruce forest surround the scenic waterfalls.

Lying next to Mirror Lake Scenic Byway, "Upper Provo River Falls" riffles down two tiers to a cold plunge pool.

"Middle Provo River Falls" forms an elegant stairstep cascade.

Two-tiered "Upper Provo River Falls," tumbling 50 feet down steep rock slabs to a chilly plunge pool, lies beyond a fenced overlook. "Middle Provo River Falls" pours 20 feet over a series of stone ledges to a clear pool lined with cliffs. "Lower Provo River Falls," seen from a viewpoint above the waterfall, plunges 35 feet in two frothy waterfalls over rocky benches to a wide pool. The trail does not descend to the base of the lower falls, so use caution if you decide to scramble down.

The frigid Provo River is usually too cold for water sports except wading on warm days, and the river runs fast with dangerous currents in early summer. Avoid slick rocks on top of the waterfalls.

More waterfalls are farther south in Slate Gorge, a deep canyon below the highway. The best place to see the Slate Gorge waterfalls is at Slate Gorge Overlook, between mileposts 22 and 23, on the east side of the road. Park in a pull-off and walk to the signed overlook high above the gorge. The muted roar of the Provo River filters up from the canyon as it plunges over several waterfalls, some as high as 50 feet, far below, including "Upper Slate Gorge Falls." Visit these waterfalls by hiking and wading up the riverbed from a bridge in late summer's low water.

Provo River Falls

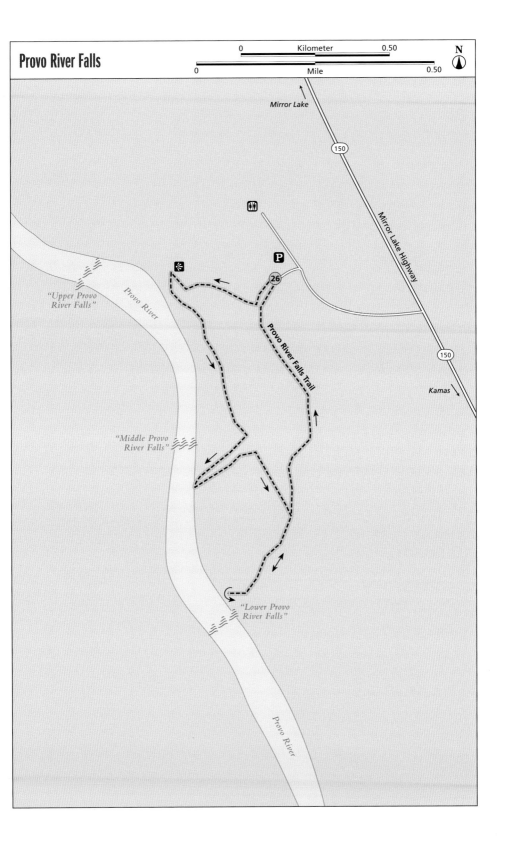

N

0   Kilometer   0.50

0   Mile   0.50

Mirror Lake

150

Mirror Lake Highway

150

Kamas

26

Provo River Falls Trail

"Upper Provo River Falls"

Provo River

"Middle Provo River Falls"

"Lower Provo River Falls"

Provo River

Provo River

"Lower Provo River Falls" drops over double bedrock benches to a deep pool.

Miles and Directions

0.0 Start at the trailhead on the southwest side of the parking lot. Go straight on a paved trail for 30 feet to a junction and go right down the paved trail and stone steps.

0.03 Reach an overlook enclosed by a stone wall and a railing with views of "Upper Provo River Falls" (GPS: 40.657529 / -110.946293). Hike south on a bench above the Provo River.

0.06 Reach a junction and go right to an overlook by "Middle Provo River Falls." Return to the junction.

0.1 Go right at the junction and hike to another junction. Keep right and continue down rocky slopes toward the river.

0.13 Reach a viewpoint above "Lower Provo River Falls" (GPS: 40.656583 / -110.946105). Return to the last junction and keep right. Continue straight to the parking lot.

0.2 Arrive back at the trailhead (GPS: 40.657484 / -110.945883).

27 "Ely Creek Falls"

Hidden in Utah's northeast corner, "Ely Creek Falls" pours over a remote cliff near Jones Hole in Dinosaur National Monument.

Start: Jones Hole Trailhead
Trails: Jones Hole Trail, Island Park Trail
Difficulty: Easy
Hiking time: 2–3 hours
Distance: 3.8 miles out and back
Elevation trailhead to falls viewpoint: 5,560 to 5,340 feet (-220 feet)
Trail surface: Dirt, sand
Restrictions: Fee area. National park rules and regulations apply. No dogs; no biking. Collecting artifacts, fossils, plants, or other objects is prohibited. Backcountry permits required for camping.
Amenities: Toilets and picnic tables at trailhead; services in Vernal
Maps: *Benchmark Maps:* Page 55 A11; Trails Illustrated #220: Dinosaur National Monument; USGS Jones Hole
County: Uintah
Land status/contact: Dinosaur National Monument, (435) 781-7700

Finding the trailhead: From the junction of US 40/Main Street and US 191/Vernal Avenue in the center of Vernal, go north on US 191 for 0.5 mile and turn right on 500 North Street. Drive east for 38.9 miles on 500 North, which becomes Brush Creek Road after leaving Vernal. Continue, following signs for Jones Hole, on Diamond Mountain Road and then Jones Hole Road. Park at a lot and trailhead at the end of the road. The trailhead is on the southwest corner of the lot (GPS: 40.587252 / -109.057045). The address is 24400 E Jones Hole, Hatchery Road, Vernal.

The Hike

South of Jones Hole National Fish Hatchery in Dinosaur National Monument, "Ely Creek Falls" spills over a 15-foot cliff shaded by tall trees. The horsetail waterfall and its plunge pool form a welcome oasis in this desert land of sandstone cliffs and canyons. Perennial water flow, arising from springs in a maze of slickrock canyons aptly named The Labyrinths, feeds the splashing waterfall a scant 0.6 mile from the Utah and Colorado border to the east.

The scenic Jones Hole Trail, beginning at the fish hatchery, follows clear, cold Jones Hole Creek down a twisting canyon walled by towering cliffs. Besides visiting the waterfall, check out the rock art on the cliff face at Deluge Rock Shelter, past a footbridge over the creek. Ancestral indigenous people created the red ocher pictographs and petroglyphs between 800 and 1,400 years ago. Look and photograph, but do not touch. Note: For more information about rock art, read *Rock Art: The Meanings and Myths Behind Ancient Ruins in the Southwest and Beyond* (FalconGuides).

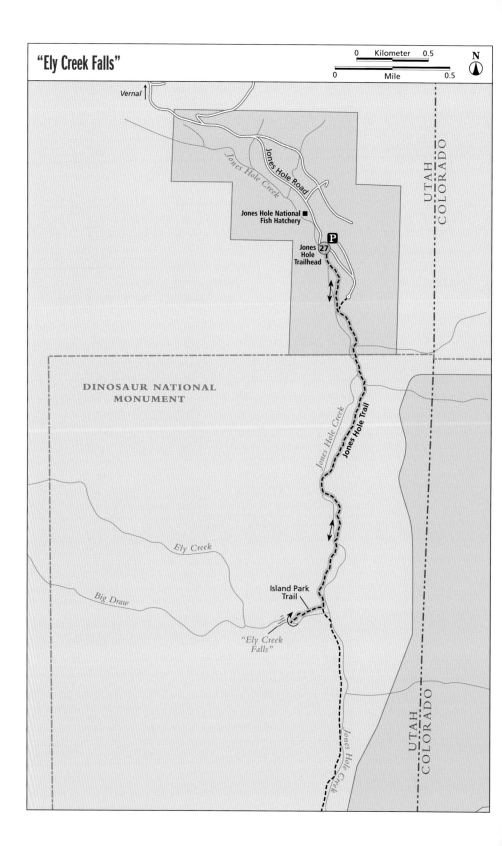

"Ely Creek Falls"

Vernal

Jones Hole Road

Jones Hole Creek

Jones Hole National ■
Fish Hatchery

P

Jones 27
Hole
Trailhead

UTAH
COLORADO

DINOSAUR NATIONAL
MONUMENT

Jones Hole Creek

Jones Hole Trail

Ely Creek

Big Draw

Island Park
Trail

"Ely Creek
Falls"

UTAH
COLORADO

Jones Hole Creek

0   Kilometer   0.5
0   Mile   0.5

N

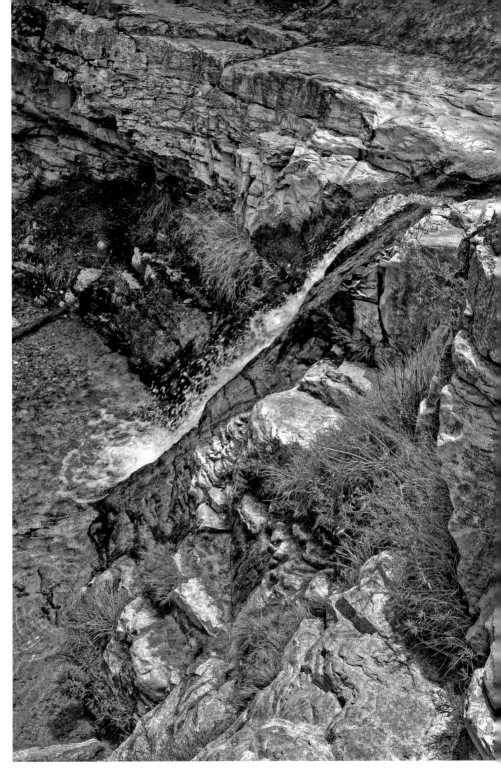

"Ely Creek Falls" riffles down a stone chute off the Jones Hole Trail.

"Ely Creek Falls" lies in a hidden garden in a sandstone side canyon in Dinosaur National Monument.

Miles and Directions

0.0 Start at the trailhead on the parking lot's southwest corner. Cross a road and hike south beside fish-rearing units.

0.2 Reach the end of the last hatchery unit (GPS: 40.584972 / -109.055912) and continue south along the east bank of Jones Hole Creek. Follow the trail down the cliff-lined canyon.

1.4 Cross the creek on a footbridge and continue south on the west bank. Past the bridge are several side trails that go right to the cliff face with panels of pictographs and petroglyphs and the Deluge Rock Shelter.

1.7 Reach a signed junction (GPS: 40.565585 / -109.057045). Go right on Island Park Trail on the north side of Ely Creek.

1.9 Arrive at "Ely Creek Falls." After a drink and snack, return along the trail.

3.8 Arrive back at the trailhead (GPS: 40.587252 / -109.057045).

Eastern Utah

Moab

Sandstone cliffs envelope Professor Creek deep in Mary Jane Canyon.

28 Mill Creek Waterfalls: "Mill Creek Falls," "Upper Mill Creek Falls," "Power Dam Falls"

A sandy trail follows Mill Creek past a waterfall over an old dam to two gorgeous waterfalls fed by a perennial creek in Mill Creek's cliff-lined North Fork Canyon.

Start: Mill Creek Canyon Trailhead
Trail: Mill Creek Trail
Difficulty: Easy, with minimal elevation gain
Hiking time: About 1 hour
Distance: 1.6 miles out and back
Elevation trailhead to falls viewpoint: 4,235 to 4,295 feet (+60 feet)
Trail surface: Sand, dirt, rock, creek crossing
Restrictions: Day use only. Limited parking at trailhead; do not park on access road. No motorized vehicles or bicycles. No buses, trailers, or RVs allowed on access road or in parking lot; parking lot vehicle length limit is 22 feet. Stay on the hiker-only trail; no glass beverage containers allowed; no camping; use ear buds to listen to music. Carry out all human and dog waste; keep pets under control; watch for poison ivy. Cliff jumping is dangerous, and serious accidents have occurred here. Do not vandalize rock art sites in the canyon; call BLM law enforcement at (435) 259-2131 to report offenders.
Amenities: Toilets at trailhead; services in Moab
Maps: *Benchmark Maps:* Page 71 G7; Trails Illustrated #507: Moab Area East (Dewey Bridge, Sand Flats); USGS Moab
County: Grand
Land status/contact: Bureau of Land Management, Moab Field Office, (435) 259-2100

Finding the trailhead: From Main Street/US 191 in downtown Moab, turn east on Center Street and drive to 400 E. Turn right and drive to Mill Creek Drive. Turn left and follow Mill Creek Drive east to its junction with Sand Flats Road on the left. Angle right on Mill Creek Road and drive 0.4 mile to Powerhouse Lane. Turn left (east) on Powerhouse and drive to its end at a large parking area and the trailhead. GPS: 38.561975 / -109.516838

The Hike

The Mill Creek Trail follows Mill Creek, a perennial stream that begins high in the La Sal Mountains, through a deep sandstone canyon east of Moab to "Mill Creek Falls" on the North Fork of Mill Creek, locally called "Left Hand Canyon." The easily accessible trail is popular in the warmer months, with scenic views, rock art panels, and swimming holes.

"Mill Creek Falls," a popular swimming hole, drops off a slickrock ledge into a deep, delicious pool.

While lovely 15-foot "Mill Creek Falls" was once a private Eden, it was discovered in the early 2000s and plastered all over the internet. Increased activity led to hundreds of people trekking back to the falls in summer, leaving trash, piles of human and dog excrement, the detritus of parties, braided social trails, and defacement of ancient rock art panels. Concerned locals began patrolling the canyon and picking up trash, while the BLM made a parking lot and instituted regulations to protect this fragile riparian ecosystem in the Mill Creek Canyon Wilderness Study Area.

It is best to avoid the trail and waterfall on weekends, busy times like spring break, and hot days, when people flock to the cool water. The trail crosses Mill Creek and the Left Fork several times, which can be difficult from November to April because the water is cold and can be deep at the fords. Water depth varies from calf-deep to thigh-deep, depending on previous flash flooding and beaver dams. It is best to hike on warm days so you can wear sandals for the crossings and can plan to get wet. While cliff jumping occurs at the waterfall, the BLM recommends not jumping from cliffs into the pool. Again, water depth varies, and serious injuries have occurred, including broken bones requiring evacuation and hospitalization.

Mill Creek Trail is susceptible to flash flooding, particularly in July and August. Watch the weather and get out of the canyon during thunderstorms. Mill Creek drains a large area, and heavy rain upstream in the La Sal Mountains can cause flooding. In the event of flooding, climb to higher ground.

The hike begins at the Mill Creek Trailhead at a large parking area at the eastern end of Powerhouse Lane, a short drive east of downtown Moab. A BLM sign with Mill Creek information and regulations marks the trail's start. The wide dirt trail heads east and after 100 yards passes a small building and the junction with Mill Creek Rim Trail, which goes right and climbs onto the canyon rim to the south. Continue to "Power Dam Falls," a human-made waterfall at the ruins on an old concrete dam that generated electrical power for Moab beginning in 1919 until a power line was built from Price to Moab in 1945. Mill Creek plunges over the top of the dam and dashes through a shallow rock-walled canyon toward Moab. This creek section is a popular summer wading spot.

Past the dam the trail scrambles across rock ledges above the creek. Beaver dams with deep pools are upstream of the dam. Restrain dogs—beavers will attack dogs that swim in their ponds. The trail enters Mill Creek Canyon below a tawny wall of Navajo Sandstone on the left and reaches the junction of Mill Creek and its North Fork. Wade across the creek and hike left on a trail up the North Fork to "Mill Creek Falls."

Extra credit: To visit "Upper Mill Creek Falls," return down the trail for a few hundred feet and turn right on a social trail that climbs to the cliff top above the creek and follows sloping sandstone slabs and shelves to the top of the lower falls. Continue hiking for 0.5 mile up the scenic canyon to the upper waterfall. Look for rock art panels about 500 feet before the first pool, between the two pools, and 500 feet past the second pool.

Mill Creek Waterfalls

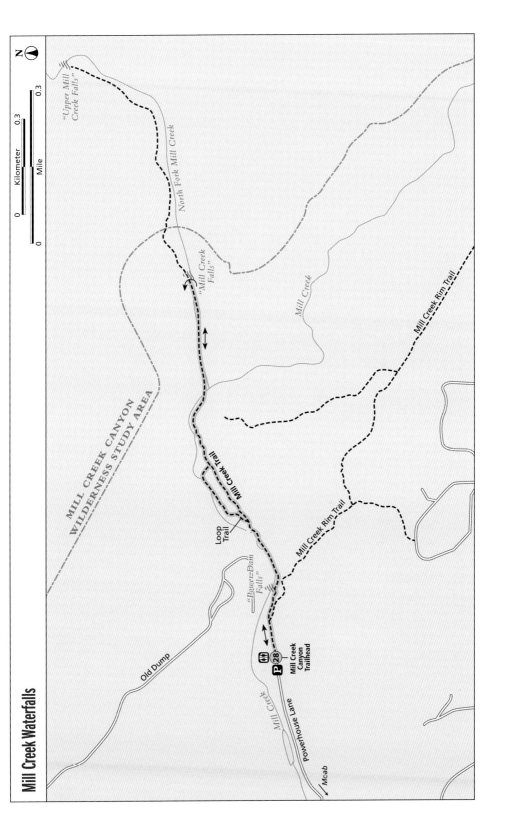

N

Kilometer
0   0.3

Mile
0   0.3

"Upper Mill Creek Falls"

North Fork Mill Creek

MILL CREEK CANYON
WILDERNESS STUDY AREA

"Mill Creek Falls"

Mill Creek

Mill Creek Rim Trail

Mill Creek Trail

Loop Trail

Mill Creek Rim Trail

"Power Dam Falls"

Old Dump

P 28
Mill Creek Canyon
Trailhead

Mill Creek

Powerhouse Lane

Mcab

Miles and Directions

0.0 Start at Mill Creek Trailhead next to the toilets. Hike east on the wide trail, with Mill Creek in a shallow gorge to the left.

0.2 Reach the ruins of an old dam and power station. "Power Dam Falls" pours over the top of the dam (GPS: 38.562102 / -109.514657). Enjoy views of the falling water from a bedrock overlook above a cliff. Hike right from the falls to a trail section that requires wading or scrambling across sandy footholds below a short cliff. Follow the trail northeast past a turn to a short loop hike that goes left to the creek and rejoins the main trail in 0.1 mile.

0.7 Hike below the shady north side of a cliff to the confluence of Mill Creek on the right and its North Fork on the left (GPS: 38.563635 / -109.507096). Go left and wade across the creek. Follow the trail up the left-fork canyon, wading the creek a couple more times and then following the creek's west bank.

0.8 Arrive at the edge of the wide pool below "Mill Creek Falls" (GPS: 38.564339 / -109.503903). After admiring the waterfall, return on the same trail.

1.4 Arrive back at the trailhead (GPS: 38.561975 / -109.516838).

◁ *The sound of desert water entices hikers to "Mill Creek Falls" on the North Fork of Mill Creek, east of Moab.*

29 "Faux Falls" and "Upper Faux Falls"

An easy hike on a loop trail leads to "Faux Falls," a gorgeous waterfall tumbling over a sandstone cliff. A short out-and-back trail leads past smaller waterfalls and cascades to "Upper Faux Falls." For extra credit, hike the nearby 0.9-mile Rock Loop Trail.

Start: Falls Loop Trailhead
Trail: Falls Loop Trail
Difficulty: Easy
Hiking time: About 1 hour
Distance: 1.3 miles round-trip to falls; 1.7 miles round-trip to upper falls
Elevation trailhead to falls viewpoint: 5,085 feet to 5,195 feet (+110 feet)
Trail surface: Dirt, sand
Restrictions: Hikers only; no mountain bikes or motorized vehicles. Stay on trails. Leashed dogs allowed. No water at trailhead.

Amenities: Toilets at trailhead; Ken's Lake Campground
Maps: *Benchmark Maps:* Page 71 H7; Trails Illustrated #507: Moab Area East (Dewey Bridge, Sand Flats); Trails Illustrated #505: Moab Greater Region; USGS Kane Springs
County: San Juan
Land status/contact: Bureau of Land Management, Moab Field Office, (435) 259-2100

Finding the trailhead: Drive south from Moab on US 191 for 7.5 miles to Ken's Lake Road (CR 175) at mile marker 117.9. Turn left (east) on Ken's Lake Road and drive 0.8 miles to a junction with La Sal Mountain Loop Road. Continue straight on CR 175 and after 1.4 miles reach a Y junction. A left turn leads to Ken's Lake. Continue straight on dirt CR 175 to a junction with the first turnoff into Ken's Lake Campground, at 1.7 miles. Continue another 0.2 mile to a left turn on Ken's Lake Campground Road on the campground's east side. Drive north on the road, passing a right turn on Faux Falls Road (4×4 track to old trailhead), for 0.2 mile to the Falls Loop Trailhead at a small parking lot on the right opposite group site B. GPS: 38.478973 / -109.419196 Alternatively, park at the start of Faux Falls Road, near the campground entrance.

The Hike

The Falls Loop Trail ends at a 45-foot waterfall that plunges off a sandstone cliff into a clear pool. The easy hike is popular in summer when hikers bask in cooling spray below the falls or wade into a 2- to 4-foot-deep pool.

The falls, named with the French word for "fake," is not a natural waterfall but rather the fortuitous result of a water diversion. "Faux Falls" is part of a project completed in 1981 that diverted water from Mill Creek to the east through a 645-foot-long tunnel in Brimley Ridge to a rocky chute and waterfall and then an unnamed

Sandstone towers etch the skyline above "Faux Falls" and ▶
"Upper Faux Falls" southeast of Moab.

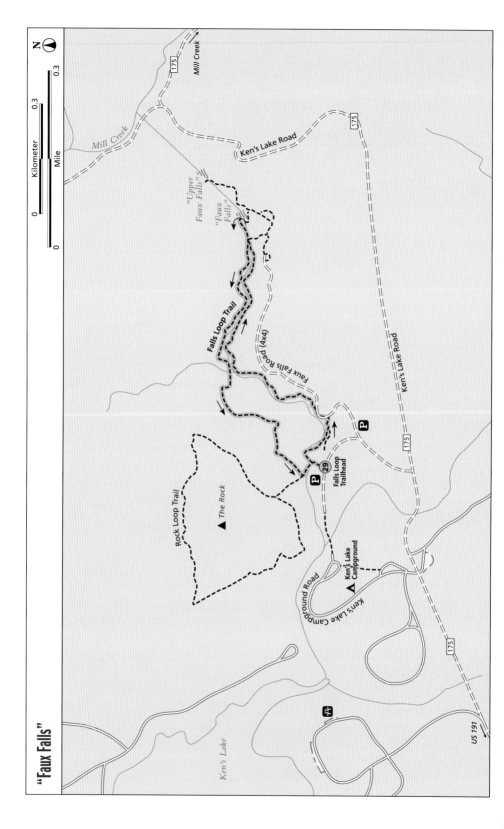

"Faux Falls"

N

0 Kilometer 0.3

0 Mile 0.3

Mill Creek

175

Mill Creek

Ken's Lake Road

175

"Upper Faux Falls"

"Faux Falls"

Falls Loop Trail

Faux Falls Road (4x4)

Ken's Lake Road

175

Rock Loop Trail

▲ The Rock

P

P

29

P

Falls Loop Trailhead

Ken's Lake Campground Road

▲ Ken's Lake Campground

175

Ken's Lake

US 191

A wilderness of sandstone surrounds "Faux Falls" on the edge of the Spanish Valley.

creek, which drains west into Ken's Lake southeast of Moab. The result is the largest waterfall in the arid Moab area.

The hike starts on the north side of the eastern loop road in Ken's Lake Campground east of the lake. The hike follows the Falls Loop Trail on an unnamed creek's south bank to "Faux Falls" and then returns to the trailhead along the north bank. Ambitious hikers can follow a sandy trail up slopes south of "Faux Falls" to view "Upper Faux Falls," a series of short waterfalls and cascades in a rocky channel. This trail ends at the creek's diversion pipe near a saddle between Mill Creek and Spanish Valley.

Extra credit: Hike the 0.9-mile Rock Loop Trail, a moderate loop around a Navajo Sandstone dome locally called "The Rock." Start at the Falls Loop Trailhead in the campground; follow the trail north and cross the creek on a bridge. Head northwest for 500 feet on an old roadbed to a junction. Go right and follow the double- and singletrack trail around The Rock to the junction. Go right and hike back to the campground and parking area.

Miles and Directions

0.0 Start at the Falls Loop Trailhead in Ken's Lake Campground. Hike north on the signed singletrack trail and descend a hill.

0.02 Reach a Y junction by the lake's unnamed inlet creek. (GPS: 38.479207 / -109.419060). Go right on Falls Loop Trail on the creek's south bank, passing a cascade left of the trail. The left-hand trail at the junction is the return trail on the creek's north side.

0.13 Reach Faux Falls Road and go left on it.

0.15 Meet a junction on the left (GPS: 38.479136 / -109.417358) and go left on Falls Loop Trail. Hike east on the creek's south bank.

0.6 Reach a junction with the return loop of Falls Loop Trail. Go right and walk 25 feet to a junction on the right, marked with a signpost. A right turn here leads to "Upper Faux Falls." Continue straight, following the sign for "Lower Faux Falls." The trail dips across the creek to the waterfall. (**Option:** Hike to "Upper Faux Falls" by following the signed out-and-back trail for 0.2 mile to the upper falls and cascades. Return to the junction for an extra 0.4-mile hike).

0.62 Arrive at the base of "Faux Falls" (GPS: 38.480973 / -109.411498). After enjoying the waterfall, return to the junction with the south bank trail.

0.7 Arrive at the south bank trail junction. Keep right on Falls Loop Trail, cross the creek, and hike west on its north bank.

1.2 Reach a T junction with Rock Loop Trail. Go left and hike southeast to a bridge over the creek.

1.25 Reach a junction at the start of the Falls Loop Trail. Go right and climb south to the campground and parking area.

1.3 Arrive back at the trailhead (GPS: 38.478973 / -109.419196).

"Faux Falls" riffles down a sandstone chute to a clear plunge pool.

30 "Professor Creek Falls"

Fed by snowmelt and springs in the La Sal Mountains, Professor Creek twists down a narrow canyon to "Professor Creek Falls," a plunge waterfall hidden in a narrow slot canyon east of Moab.

Start: Sylvester Trailhead
Trail: Professor Creek Trail
Difficulty: Moderate
Hiking time: 4–5 hours
Distance: 7.6 miles out and back
Elevation trailhead to falls viewpoint: 4,355 to 4,830 feet (+475 feet)
Trail surface: Dirt, sand, rocks, bedrock, water
Restrictions: Parking is prohibited along Professor Creek Road, only at the trailhead; no trespassing on private property along the road. No camping on access road or at trailhead. Dogs allowed but must be leashed or under voice command. Use WAG bags and pack out human and pet waste. Watch the weather, and don't hike if a storm threatens; moderate flash flood risk in the canyon.
Amenities: None at trailhead; nearby camping on River Road at Hittle Bottom, Lower Onion Creek, and Upper Onion Creek Campgrounds; services in Moab
Maps: *Benchmark Maps:* Page 71 E8, E9, F9; Trails Illustrated #507: Moab Area East (Dewey Bridge, Sand Flats); USGS Fisher Towers
County: Grand
Land status/contact: Bureau of Land Management, Moab Field Office, (435) 259-2100

Finding the trailhead: From Moab, drive north on US 191. Before the bridge over the Colorado River, turn right on UT 128/River Road and drive 20.6 miles to a right turn on unsigned Professor Creek Road/BLM 98 (GPS: 38.707268 / -109.380888). Drive south on the dirt road for 2.2 miles to the trailhead at its end. The hike starts at an unmarked trailhead left of the Sylvester Trailhead sign. GPS: 38.683719 / -109.355557

The Hike

Professor Creek, a perennial stream originating high on the north flank of the La Sal Mountains, drops through long, sinuous Mary Jane Canyon to "Professor Creek Falls." This 30-foot double-plunge waterfall rumbles off a massive boulder jam in the slot canyon below 150-foot-high sandstone walls. The hike, beginning at a trailhead at the end of a dirt ranch road, offers a superb adventure with minimal elevation gain, cool water to wade on hot days, spectacular scenery, and a hidden waterfall at trail's end.

While experienced canyoneers descend the upper canyon to a rappel at the falls, waterfall aficionados follow the trail up Professor Creek to the falls' cooling mist. The

"Professor Creek Falls" pours off jammed boulders in
Mary Jane Canyon, a narrow slot canyon east of Moab.

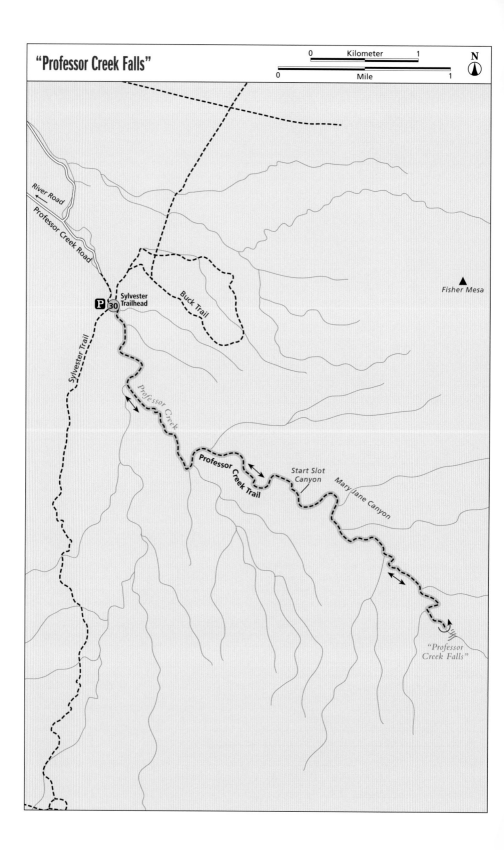

"Professor Creek Falls"

0   Kilometer   1

0   Mile   1

N

River Road

Professor Creek Road

Sylvester Trailhead

P 30

Buck Trail

Sylvester Trail

Professor Creek

Professor Creek Trail

Start Slot Canyon

Mary Jane Canyon

Fisher Mesa

"Professor Creek Falls"

Professor Creek riffles over boulders in its lower canyon below Castle Rock, The Rectory, and The Priest.

first half of the trail is easy to follow alongside the creek, with occasional crossings and magnificent views of Castle Rock—called "Castleton Tower" by climbers—The Priest, Adobe Mesa, and Fisher Mesa. The hike's second half up the slot canyon to the waterfall requires up to fifty creek crossings, depending on the creek's depth, or wading if the creek fills the canyon floor. Plan to get wet feet, so wear sandals or sturdy shoes that you will not mind getting soaked. Trekking poles are handy for balance on slippery rocks. If you have the time, investigate several dry slot canyons that veer off the main drainage.

The creek and nearby Sylvester Trail were named for Dr. Sylvester Richardson, nicknamed "The Professor." He was a medical doctor, sawmill operator, storekeeper, and county commissioner who settled in the wide valley in the 1880s with his wife, Mary Jane, who lent her name to Mary Jane Canyon. Other nearby places named for the couple include Richardson Amphitheater and Professor Valley, which the Colorado River runs through.

The canyon has moderate flash flood potential. Pay attention to the weather before setting off on your hike and watch for thunderstorms, especially in July and

August. Heavy rain in the La Sal Mountains to the south can drain quickly down the canyon, trapping hikers in the slot canyon.

Miles and Directions

0.0 Start at the trailhead by the "Professor Creek" sign and drop across a wash to a bench. Hike south along the bench on the west side of the creek with views south of jutting Adobe Mesa and west to Castle Rock, The Rectory, and The Priest.

0.3 Cross to the east bank of Professor Creek and hike southeast.

0.4 Reach the second creek crossing. Splash across the wide creek and hike along the creek's north bank.

0.6 Reach the junction with a side canyon on the right and the third creek crossing (GPS: 38.677560 / -109.353981). Follow the trail on the southeast edge of the creek to two more crossings. Plan to wade the creek many times from here, depending on water levels.

1.1 The canyon narrows, and low cliffs flank the twisting creek. This is the start of Mary Jane Canyon. Continue hiking southeast in the twisting canyon with creek crossings below high cliffs.

2.2 Towering sandstone cliffs, split by occasional side canyons and ravines, hem in the sparkling creek in a wide slot canyon. Enjoy the verdant riparian ecosystem with tall grass, reeds, willows, and cottonwood trees.

2.7 Reach an unnamed side slot canyon on the left (east) side of Mary Jane Canyon (GPS: 38.665709 / -109.331144). Scramble over a couple of boulders by the creek and continue up the main canyon, with more creek crossings.

3.8 Pass into a narrow canyon section and arrive at "Professor Creek Falls" (GPS: 38.657917 / -109.319918). Enjoy the waterfall's cool mist and the canyon's shade, then return down the canyon to the trailhead.

7.6 Arrive back at the trailhead (GPS: 38.683719 / -109.355557).

Hikers walk beside Professor Creek in cliff-lined Mary Jane Canyon.

South Central Utah

Marysville, Tropic, Torrey, Boulder, Escalante

Lower Calf Creek Falls, reached by a scenic hike, is a popular destination for waterfall lovers.

31 Bullion Falls and "Cascade Falls"

Pine Creek, originating from snowmelt on the eastern slopes of the remote Tushar Mountains, tumbles east down Bullion Canyon to a cliff band where it plunges over 70-foot Bullion Falls.

Start: Bullion Canyon Trailhead
Trail: Bullion Canyon Trail (#074)
Difficulty: Moderate
Hiking time: About 1 hour
Distance: 2 miles out and back
Elevation trailhead to falls viewpoint: 7,855 to 8,295 feet (+440 feet)
Trail surface: Dirt, rocks
Restrictions: Fee parking at trailhead. Dogs allowed. Dangerous cliffs below the waterfall viewpoint.

Amenities: None at trailhead; services in Marysvale
Maps: *Benchmark Maps:* Page 74 A5; Trails Illustrated #708: Paiute ATV Trail Map (Fish Lake National Forest/BLM); USGS Mount Brigham
County: Piute County
Land status/contact: Fishlake National Forest, (435) 896-9233; Beaver Ranger District, (435) 438-2436

Finding the trailhead: From I-70 at Siever, southeast of Richfield, take exit 23 and drive south on US 89 for 12.6 miles to Marysvale. Turn right (west) on West Bullion Avenue and drive 0.5 mile to Bullion Canyon Road (FR 126), signed for Bullion Canyon and Miners Park. Turn left and follow the road, which becomes a narrow dirt road, for 6.2 miles from US 89 to a parking area past a bridge over Pine Creek. Park in this fee lot and walk back across the bridge to the Bullion Falls Trailhead on the left. GPS: 38.414224 / -112.327362

The Hike

Fed by Pine Creek, Bullion Falls plummets into a cliff-lined gorge on the eastern flank of the Tushar Mountains, a rugged range topped by 12,169-foot Delano Peak and 12,137-foot Mount Belknap. Reach the stunning waterfall by hiking up an old road, now used by ATVs, to a side trail at Miners Park Trailhead that leads to an airy viewpoint of the horsetail waterfall. The falls are best in June, when snowmelt fills the creek.

Look for "Cascade Falls," a 60-foot waterfall tucked into an amphitheater on the south side of the canyon, from the trail before Miners Park Trailhead. The falls, best seen in early summer, is usually a trickle by August.

The ATV track ends at Miners Park Trailhead. Beyond stretches the Bullion Canyon Trail System, a network of four nonmotorized trails that explore Bullion Canyon, The Pocket, the South Fork of Pine Creek, and Delano Peak.

The hike to Bullion Falls crosses the northern edge of Miners Park, an area once riddled with gold mines and containing three towns, including Bullion City, which boasted a population of 1,651 in the 1881 census. Gold, discovered here in 1865, led

Bullion Falls and "Cascade Falls"

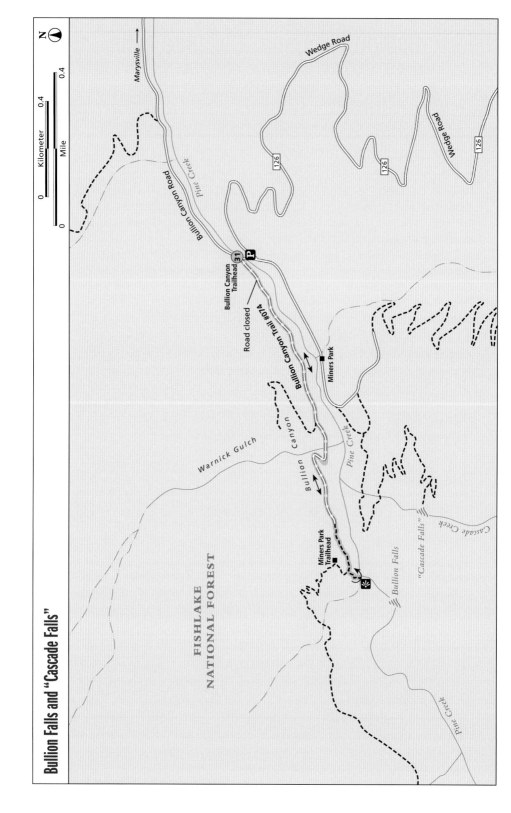

Dashing down a steep canyon on the east flank of the Tushar Mountains, Pine Creek drops over a cliff at Bullion Falls.

to a rush of prospectors and merchants seeking fame and fortune. After visiting Bullion Falls, explore this rich mining history by following the Canyon of Gold Auto Tour, a self-guided auto trip maintained by Fishlake National Forest. An informative brochure is available at a kiosk at the tour's starting point in the lower canyon. Stops along the route include Witt Tate Mine, Dalton Mill and Boardinghouse, Bullion City townsite, Bully Boy Mill, and Miners Park Historical Trail.

Miles and Directions

0.0 Begin at the Bullion Canyon Trailhead (signed for Bullion Falls) on the north side of the bridge over Pine Creek. Hike west on Bullion Canyon Trail, a 4×4 road.

0.3 Reach a crumbling log cabin on the right side of the trail. Continue straight.

0.5 Reach an old road on the right that climbs to an abandoned mine. Continue straight on the road/trail.

0.6 Reach a switchback.

0.7 Pass a signed viewpoint that looks south to "Cascade Falls" in a cliff-lined amphitheater (GPS: 38.410956 / -112.338344).

Misty water at Bullion Falls waters moss, ferns, and flowers in a nineteenth-century mining district.

0.9 Reach an info kiosk at the Miners Park Trailhead and a trail junction (GPS: 38.410063 / -112.342177). Go left on a side singletrack trail signed for Bullion Falls. The main singletrack trail (road ends here) heads right and continues into upper Bullion Canyon.

1.0 Arrive at an airy overlook of Bullion Falls (GPS: 38.409594 / -112.342508). Use caution—cliffs drop below the viewpoint. After admiring the waterfall, return down the trail. To reach the base of the falls, continue down steep slopes to a rock-rimmed pool.

2.0 Arrive back at the trailhead (GPS: 38.414224 / -112.327362).

32 "Mossy Cave Falls"

This roaring desert waterfall, on the northeastern edge of Bryce Canyon National Park, lies along a perennial stream in Water Canyon, a hoodoo-lined gorge north of Tropic.

Start: Mossy Cave Trailhead
Trail: Mossy Cave Trail
Difficulty: Easy
Hiking time: About 1 hour
Distance: 0.8 mile out and back
Elevation trailhead to falls viewpoint: 6,825 to 6,905 feet (+80 feet)
Trail surface: Dirt
Restrictions: Fee area (keep pass or proof of admission with vehicle). No pets allowed. Not an accessible trail. Stay on the trail to protect fragile rock formations and delicate plants. Respect closure signs. The area is busy between 10 a.m. and 6 p.m. in summer; if parking lot is full, return later in the day. No parking along UT 12; illegally parked cars are ticketed.
Amenities: Accessible restrooms at trailhead; services in Tropic
Maps: *Benchmark Maps:* Page 83 A7; Trails Illustrated #219: Bryce Canyon National Park; USGS: Tropic Canyon
County: Garfield
Land status/contact: Bryce Canyon National Park, (435) 834-5322

Finding the trailhead: From a roundabout at the junction of UT 12 and UT 63, which goes south to Bryce Canyon National Park, continue east on UT 12. Drive 3.7 miles, descending a long hill, to the parking lot at Mossy Cave Trailhead on the right (west) side of the highway. (GPS: 37.665772 / -112.110320). If the lot is full, do not park along the highway shoulder.

The Hike

Fed by Tropic Reservoir on the Paunsaugunt Plateau above the Pink Cliffs, the East Fork of the Sevier River meanders north before most of its water is diverted into Tropic Ditch and down Water Canyon, where it rushes over a bench of hard dolomite as "Mossy Cave Falls," also called "Tropic Ditch Falls." The 25-foot waterfall free-falls off an overhanging cliff before dashing down the canyon and past the trailhead.

The waterfall did not naturally occur in this dry canyon but formed after Mormon settlers used shovels and picks between 1890 and 1892 to excavate Tropic Ditch, an irrigation canal diverting water from the Siever River on the plateau to the west into the canyon. The precious water still irrigates fields and pastures surrounding the small town of Tropic to the south.

Like Bryce Amphitheater to the south, erosion has chiseled strange hoodoos, fins, and buttresses on Water Canyon's orange-tinged slopes. To protect the fragile geologic features and easily eroded slopes, stay on the trail; do not scramble up to the hoodoos. In addition to the waterfall, also visit Mossy Cave by following a short, steep trail that cuts left just before the falls. It ends at a wide alcove roofed by Claron Limestone. Water seeps from the ceiling, forming a hanging garden of moss and ferns in summer

"Mossy Cave Falls"

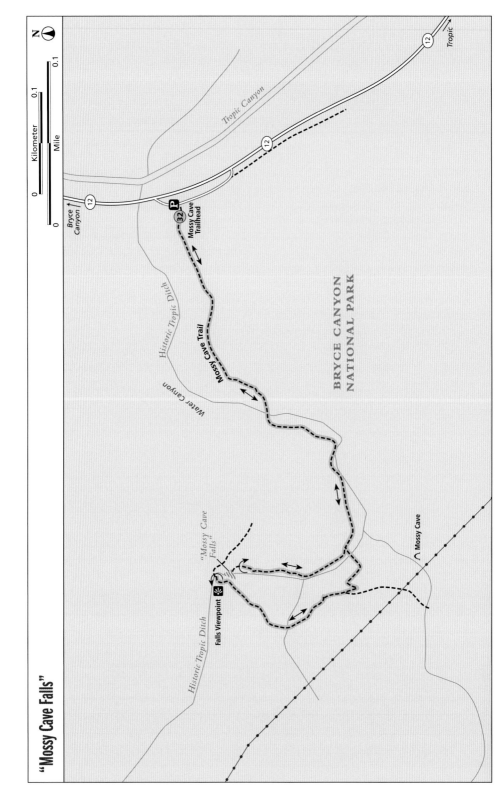

N

Kilometer
0   0.1   0.1

Mile
0   0.1

Bryce
Canyon ←

12

Tropic Canyon

12

12

Tropic

Mossy Cave Trailhead

32

P

Historic Tropic Ditch

Water Canyon

Mossy Cave Trail

BRYCE CANYON
NATIONAL PARK

∧ Mossy Cave

"Mossy Cave Falls"

Falls Viewpoint

Historic Tropic Ditch

"Mossy Cave Falls," on the east edge of Bryce Canyon National Park, plunges off a ruddy cliff into a shallow pool.

and thick icicles in winter. Do not enter the alcove—the base is muddy, and delicate plants are easily damaged. Instead, enjoy its lushness from a viewpoint at the trail's end.

Miles and Directions

0.0 Start from the trailhead and hike west across a terrace on the south side of the creek.

0.15 Cross a bridge over the creek and continue west along its north bank.

0.25 Reach a second bridge and cross to the creek's west bank. Climb steeper slopes past the bridge and continue northwest above a shallow cliff-lined gorge. Pass a junction with a trail that goes left to Mossy Cave, a leafy grotto 0.1 mile up that trail. Continue to a waterfall overlook with an information sign at 0.3 mile. Use caution at this unfenced point. Continue hiking north above the gorge.

0.4 Reach the top of "Mossy Cave Falls" (GPS: 37.665461 / -112.114356). Sandstone slabs above the falls are slick, so be cautious if you wade into the creek. After enjoying the rush of water, return down the trail.

0.8 Arrive back at the trailhead (GPS: 37.665772 / -112.110320).

Extra credit: To visit the base of "Mossy Cave Falls," go right before crossing the bridge and hike up a rough trail along the right side of the creek for 0.1 mile. Depending on water levels, some wading may be required.

33 Sulphur Creek Waterfalls: "Upper Sulphur Creek Falls," "Middle Sulphur Creek Falls," "Lower Sulphur Creek Falls"

Three desert waterfalls—12-foot "Upper Sulphur Creek Falls," 12-foot "Middle Sulphur Creek Falls," and 6-foot "Lower Sulphur Creek Falls"—hide in the narrows of Sulphur Creek Canyon in the heart of Capitol Reef National Park.

Start: Sulphur Creek Trailhead
Trail: Sulphur Creek Trail
Difficulty: Moderate
Hiking time: 3-4 hours
Distance: 6.0 miles point to point
Elevation trailhead to falls: 6,090 to 5,495 feet (-595 feet)
Trail surface: Dirt, sand, bedrock
Restrictions: National park regulations apply; no dogs or bikes. Follow existing trails; do not build cairns or build dams in creek. Pack out trash; dispose of human waste properly, or use a WAG bag, RESTOP, or other portable toilet kit and pack it out. Do not scratch, paint, or damage rock surfaces. High flash-flood risk in the canyons; watch the weather, and don't hike if a storm threatens. Follow Leave No Trace principles.
Amenities: None at trailhead; restrooms and water at visitor center; nearby campgrounds; services in Torrey
Maps: Benchmark Maps: Page 76 B3; Trails Illustrated #267: Capitol Reef National Park; USGS Twin Rocks
County: Wayne
Land status/contact: Capitol Reef National Park, (435) 425-3791

Finding the trailhead: From the Capitol Reef National Park Visitor Center, drive west on UT 24 for 3.3 miles (0.3 mile past Chimney Rock Trailhead) to Sulphur Creek Trailhead on the left (south) side of the highway. The signed trailhead is on the south side of the parking lot (GPS: 38.317147 / -111.308936). The hike ends at an informal trailhead by the park visitor center. GPS: 38.291391 / -111.261685

If you have a shuttle vehicle to return to the trailhead, park north of the visitor center at a pull-off on the right (north) side of the highway before a bridge over Sulphur Creek.

The Hike

Sulphur Creek, beginning on the southern edge of Meeks Mesa to the northeast, twists down a long cliff-lined canyon before emptying into the Fremont River in Capitol Reef National Park. The most spectacular section of the deep canyon includes five bends through The Goosenecks, a 2-mile section of narrows, and three waterfalls:

"Upper Sulphur Creek Falls" splashes noisily down a
sandstone tongue into an inner gorge.

"Upper Sulphur Creek Falls," "Middle Sulphur Creek Falls," and "Lower Sulphur Creek Falls." An unmaintained trail starts on UT 24, descends into a dry canyon, and then follows perennial Sulphur Creek to the park visitor center.

The unofficial trail, not recommended for beginner hikers, requires route-finding skills in a couple spots, walking through water that ranges from ankle to waist deep, and the skills to bypass a couple of waterfalls by scrambling down 12-foot drops. Depending on weather conditions, some water sections may require swimming. Due to uneven footing and deep, fast water, small children should not attempt this hike. Ask at the visitor center for current conditions.

The hike is usually done one way, from the upper trailhead to the visitor center. This requires leaving a shuttle vehicle at each end of the trail or hiking 3.3 miles up UT 24 to the upper trailhead and parking lot.

The hike's greatest danger is flash flooding. Do not hike Sulphur Creek if there is any chance of rain. The canyon carries a moderate to high risk of flash flooding, especially in summer, when heavy thunderstorms regularly drop heavy rain upstream. While it might not rain in the canyon, rainfall more than 10 miles up the canyon can flood it. Pay attention when hiking for clues that a flash flood is a possibility, including rising water levels, changes in the water's color, and thunderclaps to the west. Look for escape routes to higher ground.

Caution: Because *E. coli* bacteria are found in the stream, do not drink or ingest water from Sulphur Creek. Runoff from cattle pastures, agricultural land, and wildlife and human waste to the west contaminates the water.

Miles and Directions

0.0 Start at the trailhead, signed "Visitor Center Via Sulphur Creek." Hike south, gently descending dry slopes.

0.1 Reach a dry wash and go left. Hike down the wash past cliffs and occasional views of Chimney Rock. As the trail descends, cliffs rise higher above the narrowing canyon. After 1.75 miles, reach a narrow section and downclimb two 6-foot steps. Continue down the wash.

1.85 Meet Sulphur Creek and go left (GPS: 38.303584 / -111.304330). Hike down the stream, crossing it by wading or stepping on rocks, through the deepening canyon through a section of five bends called The Goosenecks. After hiking about 0.5 mile from the junction, look up 800 feet to spot the railing at Goosenecks Overlook and tourists looking down. Continue along and through the creek below cliffs.

3.3 Follow the creek, bending right, and enter a rock-walled canyon and the top of "Upper Sulphur Creek Falls" (GPS: 38.294777 / -111.293875) at the start of a narrow section. Pass the waterfall on the right by following a sloping ledge system above the creek and then downclimbing about 10 feet down to the creek. Wade down the creek in a slot canyon, which opens and then pinches down to a 5-foot gap (3.35 miles). Wade or swim through the pool here, depending on water levels, and continue down the canyon.

3.4 Arrive at the top of "Middle Sulphur Creek Falls" (GPS: 38.294344 / -111.292021). Pass the waterfall on the right, crossing a slickrock slab above the creek, scrambling through a hole, and downclimbing rock steps to the creek. Wade and boulder hop down a long narrow section.

Sulphur Creek Waterfalls

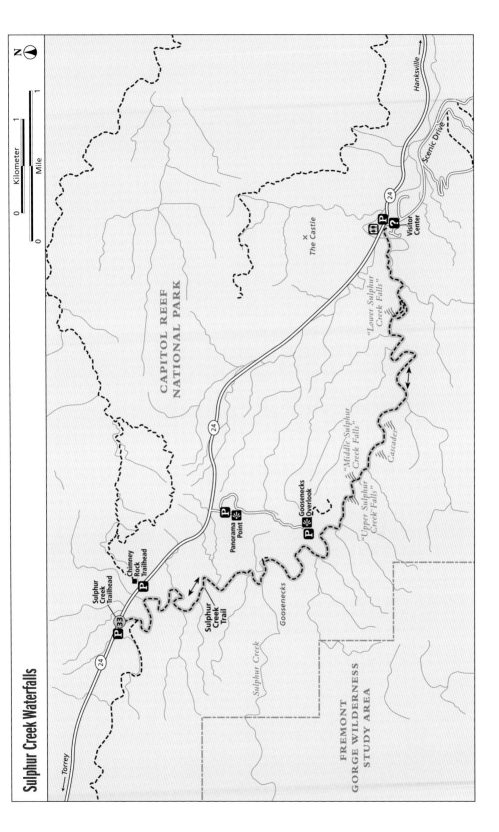

Sulphur Creek forms a deep rock-walled channel below "Middle Sulphur Creek Falls."

3.55 Pass a cascade where the creek riffles over a bedrock ledge. Continue down the canyon.

3.8 Reach a long cascade with the creek dashing down sandstone slabs. Hike down the cliff-lined canyon to another cascade.

5.0 Arrive at the top of "Lower Sulphur Creek Falls" (GPS: 38.290543 / -111.272034), which slides down a bedrock canyon and pours into a large pool. It is possible to pass the falls and pool on the left by traversing sloping rock to a tricky downclimb. Alternatively, slide down the falls and wade or swim across the pool, depending on its depth. The best way to pass the falls is to go upstream for 60 feet and climb rock steps out of the canyon. Looking for cairns, hike the slope to a narrow bypass trail that heads east across slopes above a cliff and the pool and then descends to the main trail below the cliff-lined canyon.

5.2 Reach Sulphur Creek (GPS: 38.289967 / -111.270308) and hike left up the canyon to the pool and third waterfall. Enjoy the view, then return to the junction. Hike down the wide canyon on the creek's south side below cliffs to a crossing, then follow the north side to another creek crossing.

5.7 Reach a sign pointing left that says, "Trail Visitor Center." Cross the creek and follow the trail past a historic limekiln ruin and across open terrain. Drop down and cross the creek to the back side of the visitor center. Follow the trail left around the visitor center's north side.

6.0 Arrive at an informal trailhead at the north end of the parking lot in front of the visitor center (GPS: 38.291391 / -111.261685).

Option: If you do not want to hike the canyon, take a 2.0-mile out-and-back hike to "Lower Sulphur Creek Falls." Begin at the north end of the visitor center parking lot, follow the trail around the center, and cross Sulphur Creek. Continue west on the trail up the canyon to the waterfall and pool. Return on the trail to the visitor center trailhead.

34 "Singletree Falls"

"Singletree Falls," reached by a short hike from Singletree Campground, is a two-tiered waterfall that splashes over a sandstone cliff in a verdant canyon on the eastern slope of Boulder Mountain, south of Torrey.

Start: Singletree Falls Trailhead
Trail: Singletree Falls Trail (#35157)
Difficulty: Moderate
Hiking time: About 1 hour
Distance: 1.0 mile out and back
Elevation trailhead to falls viewpoint: 8,250 to 8,005 feet (-245 feet)
Trail surface: Dirt, rocks
Restrictions: Leashed dogs only in campground. No ATVs or OHVs in campground.

Amenities: Singletree Campground; flush and vault toilets; drinking water; services in Torrey
Maps: *Benchmark Maps:* Page 76 C2; Trails Illustrated #267: Capitol Reef National Park; USGS Grover
County: Wayne
Land status/contact: Dixie National Forest, (435) 896-9233; Fremont Ranger District, (435) 836-2800

Finding the trailhead: From the junction of UT 24 and UT 12 on the east side of Torrey, turn south on UT 12. Drive 11.8 miles to a left turn onto FR 30537, signed "Singletree Campground," on the highway's east side. Drive 0.3 mile to a Y junction and go right; park in a small lot opposite the campground host's site (GPS: 38.161962 / -111.331721). The Singletree Falls Trailhead is on the south side of the parking area. When the campground is closed in the off-season, park off the highway and hike the road to the trailhead.

The Hike

Rising on the northeastern flank of broad Boulder Mountain, Singletree Creek twists through thick evergreen woods to Scenic Byway 12, an All-American Road that offers spectacular scenery, Singletree Campground, and then drops to 75-foot "Singletree Falls." Reach the two-tiered, horsetail waterfall by a 0.5-mile hike that descends into a canyon east of the campground. The first half of Singletree Falls Trail is mellow, but the second half descends steeply to the waterfall's base. The falls are best in May and June, when snowmelt swells the creek. The falls run year-round, although creek flows might be meager during prolonged dry spells.

The trail begins at Singletree Campground, one of the largest public campgrounds in the area. The campground offers excellent overnight stays and, at an elevation of 8,200 feet, cooler temperatures than nearby Capitol Reef National Park. If the campground is open, check with the camp host across the road from the trailhead to see if you need to pay a day-use fee.

Singletree Creek, originating on Boulder Mountain, drops east to "Singletree Falls" south of Torrey.

"Singletree Falls"

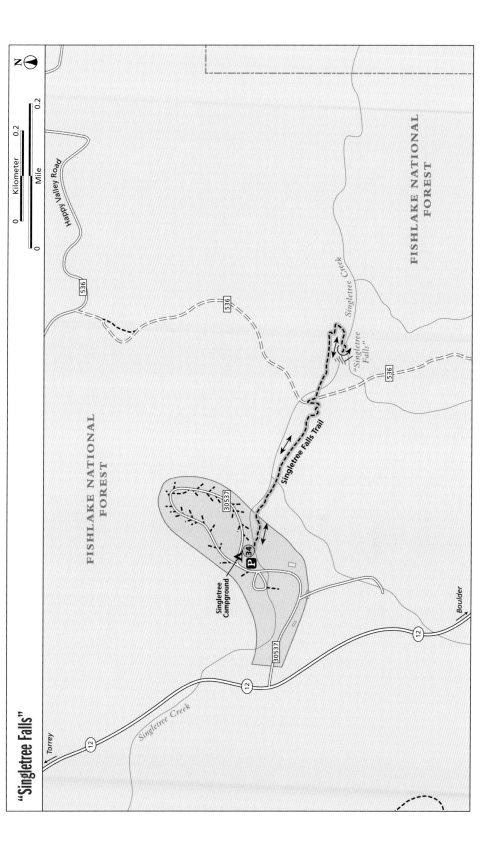

Singletree Falls Trail offers distant views of the Henry Mountains and the Twin Peaks.

Miles and Directions

0.0   Start at the Singletree Falls Trailhead. Cross a boardwalk over Singletree Creek and hike southeast through ponderosa pine woods along the southern edge of the campground.

0.1   Reach a barbed-wire fence and gate. Pass through the gate, remembering to close it, and continue southeast on the trail. Descend a rocky slope covered with sagebrush and tall pines, with good views east of sandstone domes and the Henry Mountains.

0.25 Reach FR 536, a four-wheel-drive track, and go right. Hike 50 feet to a trail junction on the left (GPS: 38.160573 / -111.327751). Go left on Singletree Falls Trail and cross a footbridge in an aspen grove. Continue down the steeper trail into a canyon.

0.4   At a signed trail junction in the bottom of the canyon (GPS: 38.159975 / -111.326111), go right and hike toward the sound of the waterfall. Singletree Falls Trail goes left here and descends to Happy Valley.

0.5   Arrive at the base of "Singletree Falls" (GPS: 38.160004 / -111.326579). After enjoying the falls, return up the trail, gaining 245 feet of elevation.

1.0   Arrive back at the trailhead (GPS: 38.161962 / -111.331721).

35 Lower Calf Creek Falls

Reached by a scenic hike up a verdant desert canyon, showy Lower Calf Creek Falls leaps off a streaked and polished sandstone cliff into a cold plunge pool in the cul-de-sac canyon.

Start: Lower Calf Creek Falls Trailhead
Trail: Lower Calf Creek Falls Trail
Difficulty: Moderate
Hiking time: 3–4 hours
Distance: 6.0 miles out and back
Elevation trailhead to falls viewpoint: 5,345 to 5,550 feet (+205 feet)
Trail surface: Dirt, sand, rocks
Restrictions: Fee area. Parking is limited at trailhead; do not park on entrance road to trailhead; no trailers or camping allowed at trailhead parking lot. No camping in canyon or at the waterfall. No garbage service; pack out all trash; bury human waste or use a WAG bag, RESTOP, or other portable toilet kit. Leashed dogs only; pick up and pack out all dog waste to protect the watershed. Wear waterproof sunscreen to minimize water contamination.

No campfires or firearms. Do not stack rocks. No rappelling. Do not touch rock art or climb in ruins; collecting is prohibited. Watch the weather to avoid flash floods.
Amenities: Vault toilets at trailhead; potable water at trailhead Apr through Oct; Calf Creek Campground; services in Escalante and Boulder
Maps: *Benchmark Maps:* Page 76 G1, G2; Trails Illustrated #710: Canyons of the Escalante (Grand Staircase-Escalante National Monument); USGS Calf Creek
County: Garfield
Land status/contact: Grand Staircase-Escalante National Monument, (435) 644-1200; Escalante Interagency Visitor Center, (435) 826-5499

Finding the trailhead: Calf Creek Recreation Area and the trailhead are located off UT 12. From the junction of UT 12 and Burr Trail Road on the south side of Boulder, drive south on UT 12 for 11.3 miles to a right turn to the recreation area, trailhead, and parking lot. From the junction of Main Street and Center Street in Escalante, drive northeast for 15.6 miles to a left turn to the trailhead. Follow the campground road for 0.2 mile to a parking lot and toilets (GPS: 37.793690 / -111.414999). The trailhead is 0.4 mile up the road from the parking lot. GPS: 37.795723 / -111.413642

The Hike

Arising from springs in the White Cliffs, a landscape of petrified sand dunes, perennial Calf Creek twists 1.0 mile to Upper Calf Creek Falls, then follows its inner gorge for another 3.0 miles to a sharp notch where Lower Calf Creek Falls plunges 126 feet into a cliff-walled pocket. The sound of falling water and the lush greenery along Calf Creek form a dramatic juxtaposition with the surrounding dry land of little rain, few permanent streams, and gleaming sandstone domes and cliffs. Dripping springs on the smooth cliffs around Lower Calf Creek Falls nurture hanging gardens of maidenhair

Lower Calf Creek Falls Trail follows a perennial creek up a canyon lined with Navajo Sandstone cliffs.

fern and columbine, while a shady forest of birch, cottonwood, box elder, and Gambel oak fills the canyon floor below the falls.

Passing Navajo Sandstone cliffs, beaver ponds lined with willows, granaries for storing seeds and red ocher pictographs made by Ancestral Puebloans, and a verdant riparian ecosystem, a pleasant trail winds up the canyon to the waterfall, one of the iconic attractions in Grand Staircase–Escalante National Monument. A brochure, keyed to fifteen numbered posts along the trail, explains the canyon's natural history, geologic features, and prehistory, educates your hike. Pick up a brochure from the campground host, at the visitor center in Escalante, or download it from the BLM website.

The waterfall has long been a popular off-the-beaten-highway attraction, but the success of Utah's Mighty Five ad campaign inundated the site with visitors. Plan to get an early start and you might have the falls to yourself. Later in the day, the waterfall area, especially on weekends and holidays, is jammed with people cooling off in the deep plunge pool. With increased visitation, practice a Leave No Trace ethic; follow existing trails, pick up trash, properly dispose of human and dog waste, and take

One of Utah's iconic waterfalls, Lower Calf Creek Falls plunges 126 feet into a cliff-walled box canyon.

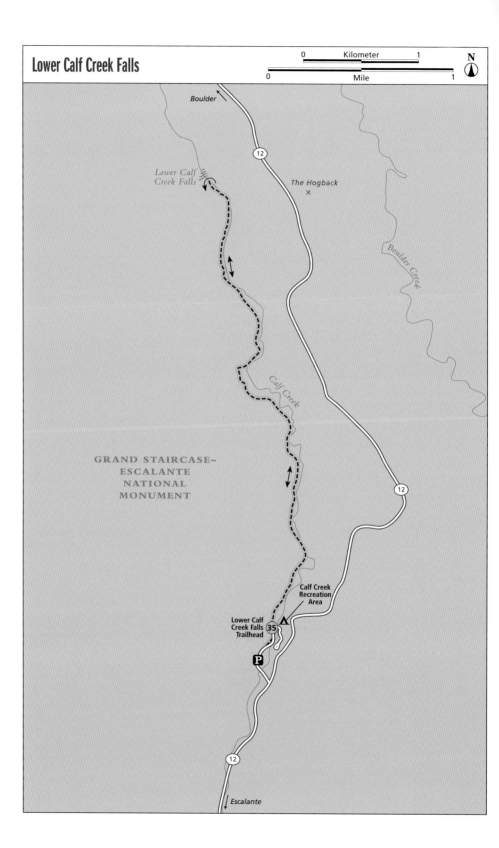

Lower Calf Creek Falls

Boulder

12

Lower Calf
Creek Falls

The Hogback
×

Boulder Creek

Calf Creek

GRAND STAIRCASE–
ESCALANTE
NATIONAL
MONUMENT

12

Calf Creek
Recreation
Area

Lower Calf
Creek Falls
Trailhead   35

P

12

Escalante

only photographs. If you swim or wade in the pool, wear waterproof sunscreen to avoid polluting the water and contaminating downstream ecosystems.

Miles and Directions

0.0 Start at the parking lot on the campground road. Walk north up the road. Before the road dips across Calf Creek, look left for the trailhead.

0.15 Reach the signed trailhead on the left side of the road (GPS: 37.795692 / -111.413660). Walk up the trail to a sign detailing rules and regulations, desert hiking safety, and trail etiquette and a trail register. After signing the register, hike north on the wide, well-marked trail, crossing open rocky areas, sections of sand, and through scrubby woods on the creek's floodplain. High cliffs, split by side drainages, line the canyon walls.

1.75 On a bend, the trail follows a high bluff above the wide canyon floor filled with dense willow thickets and beaver ponds that prevent flooding, nurture trout, and provide habitat for birds and animals.

1.8 Dip across a side drainage. From post number 6 (GPS: 37.815032 / -111.417534), look across to the side canyon's right side. Tucked on a ledge below the cliff are a couple masonry granaries built by Ancestral Puebloans more than 800 years ago. There are a couple pictograph panels across the main canyon, but they are difficult to spot without binoculars. Continue hiking on the trail, which passes beneath a towering cliff and bends into a lush, narrow canyon. Hike up the canyon beside gurgling Calf Creek.

3.0 Reach a wide plunge pool and thundering Lower Calf Creek Falls at a sandy beach and shady water birch forest (GPS: 37.828890 / -111.420098). Grab a log or sit on the beach to enjoy the sound and smell of desert water. After a long drink of water and a sandwich, return south on the trail.

6.0 Arrive back at the official trailhead (GPS: 37.795723 / -111.413642). Walk down the road to the parking lot.

6.15 Arrive back at the parking lot (GPS: 37.793690 / -111.414999).

36 Upper Calf Creek Falls

A short, steep trail descends sandstone slabs and slopes from a high mesa to Calf Creek's cliff-lined inner canyon and a majestic 87-foot waterfall that plunges through empty space to a broad pool lined with trees and dense vegetation, forming a verdant desert oasis.

Start: Upper Calf Creek Falls Trailhead
Trail: Upper Calf Creek Falls Trail
Difficulty: Moderate
Hiking time: About 2 hours
Distance: 2.0 miles out and back
Elevation trailhead to falls viewpoint: 6,520 to 5,870 feet (-650 feet)
Trail surface: Dirt, sand, rocks, slickrock
Restrictions: Limited parking at the trailhead. Hiker-only trail; maximum group size is twelve. No campfires or firearms. Pack out all trash; bury human waste or use a WAG bag, RESTOP, or other portable toilet kit. Leashed dogs only; pick up and pack out dog waste to protect the watershed. Do not stack rocks; do not touch rock art or climb in ruins; collecting is prohibited. Wear waterproof sunscreen to minimize water contamination and protect Calf Creek's ecosystems. Watch the weather to avoid flash floods.
Amenities: None at trailhead; services in Escalante and Boulder
Maps: *Benchmark Maps:* Page 76 F1; Trails Illustrated #710: Canyons of the Escalante (Grand Staircase-Escalante National Monument); USGS Calf Creek
County: Garfield
Land status/contact: Grand Staircase-Escalante National Monument, (435) 644-1200

Finding the trailhead: The trailhead and parking lot are located off the west side of UT 12. From the junction of UT 12 and Burr Trail Road on the south side of Boulder, drive south on UT 12 for 5.6 miles to an unmarked right turn to the trailhead. From the junction of Main and Center Streets in Escalante, drive northeast on UT 12 for 21.3 miles to an unmarked left turn to the trailhead. Follow the dirt road for 0.08 mile (450 feet) to a parking lot and the trailhead. GPS: 37.859452 / -111.437878

The Hike

Upper Calf Creek Falls, 3 miles north up a twisting inner gorge from its famous twin, Lower Calf Creek Falls, pours off a rounded notch and free-falls 87 feet into a spacious, overhanging amphitheater composed of pale Navajo Sandstone. Lush vegetation and trees, including cottonwoods, willow, and birch, surround the wide pool below the waterfall, providing habitat for birds and wildlife; hanging gardens of ferns and flowers adorn the alcove walls.

Upper Calf Creek Falls free-falls 87 feet into a deep ▶
plunge pool in a sandstone amphitheater.

The trail to Upper Calf Creek Falls descends to the canyon's cliff-lined inner gorge.

Compared to the lower falls, Upper Calf Creek Falls has fewer visitors, especially since the trail is rougher and loses almost 700 feet of elevation, which must be regained on the hike out. Besides solitude, the hike offers eye-grabbing scenery and a second bonus waterfall hidden in a smaller alcove above the main event. (Note: See the extra credit description below for details on finding "Calf Creek Pool Falls.")

The trail to Upper Calf Creek Falls begins from a trailhead atop flat New Home Bench, south of Boulder. The first 0.25 mile descends a sandstone slab that is easier than it looks. Cairns mark the trail, and the footing is secure. This section is the crux of the hike out—it bakes in sunlight. The last trail section into the waterfall's alcove follows a wide ledge system above the inner canyon. The tricky part is a short downclimb over a boulder by a juniper. In the thick foliage below the waterfall, watch for thickets of poison ivy, with plants up to 4 feet high. Identify it by looking for shiny green leaves in groups of three.

Miles and Directions

0.0 Start at the trailhead on the parking lot's west side. Walk 115 feet west to a registration box and a sign with information on rules, regulations, and desert safety. Continue down an open slope with scattered junipers and then descend a sandstone slab (Class 2 hiking). Look for occasional cairns to keep you on the trail.

Upper Calf Creek Falls

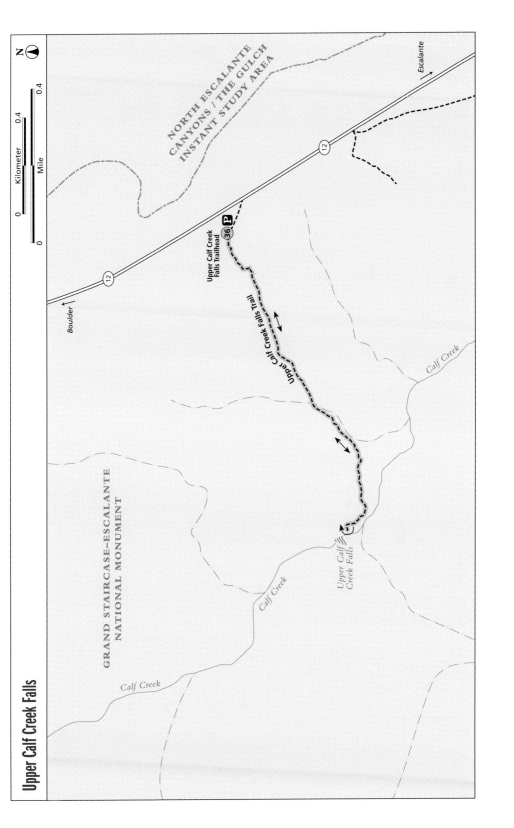

The miracle of flowing water at Upper Calf Creek Falls provides welcome shade, dense under-growth, and birdsong.

0.25 Reach the end of a sandstone tongue (GPS: 37.858006 / -111.441496). Take note of this spot so you can find it on the hike out. Follow the dirt trail west, gently descending across dry slopes with junipers and slickrock slabs. Near the canyon rim, the trail bends right and follows the rimrock.

0.8 Reach a Y junction and keep left (GPS: 37.854382 / -111.449705). Follow the trail down sandstone slabs to the canyon's edge.

0.85 Continue on the trail, heading north across a ledge system above the canyon into the vaulting alcove surrounding Upper Calf Creek Falls. There's a shady view of the falls from a ledge high on the east side of the alcove.

1.0 Descend a narrow trail to the edge of a large pool surrounded by thick vegetation below the waterfall. Watch for poison ivy along the trail. After enjoying the falling water, retrace your steps out of the alcove.

1.2 Return to the junction with the rim trail and keep right. Follow the rising trail east to the base of the final slickrock slab. Climb the slab, following cairns, back to the canyon rim.

2.0 Arrive back at the trailhead (GPS: 37.859452 / -111.437878).

Extra credit: To see "Calf Creek Pool Falls," hike to the junction at 0.8 mile and take the right trail. Follow it along the canyon rim to the top of the main waterfall and a large pool above its pour-off. Continue across slabs above the creek for another 250 feet to another deep pool and a lovely waterfall dashing about 50 feet off a cliff (GPS: 37.855802 / -111.452533).

Southwest Utah

Parowan, Cedar City, Kanarraville, St. George, Springdale, Hildale

Falling like spun silk, Kanarra Creek plunges over its namesake waterfall.

37 "Hidden Haven Falls"

"Hidden Haven Falls," fed by Benson Creek, tumbles 65 feet off a vertical cliff below the creek's narrow upper canyon into a deep valley carved by Parowan Creek.

Start: Hidden Haven Trailhead
Trail: Hidden Haven Trail
Difficulty: Easy
Hiking time: About 1 hour
Distance: 1.6 miles out and back
Elevation trailhead to falls viewpoint: 7,165 to 7,285 feet (+120 feet)
Trail surface: Dirt, gravel, rock
Restrictions: Dogs not allowed

Amenities: None; services in Parowan
Maps: *Benchmark Maps:* Page 74 G1; Trails Illustrated #702: Cedar City, Markagunt Plateau; USGS Parowan
County: Iron
Land status/contact: Parowan Canyon Wildlife Management Area, Utah Division of Natural Resources, (435) 865-6100

Finding the trailhead: From I-15 on the north side of Parowan, take exit 78. Drive south on Main Street/UT 274 to Center Street and turn left (east). Drive 3 blocks to an intersection with 300 E and South Canyon Roads. Angle right on South Canyon Road, which becomes UT 143, toward Brian Head. Set your odometer here and drive 5.6 miles to a parking lot on the left for the Parowan Canyon Wildlife Management Area and Hidden Haven Trailhead. GPS: 37.772194 / -112.840326

The Hike

Benson Creek, rising from snowmelt and springs on the north slope of 11,307-foot Brian Head, drops northwest down a steep cliff-walled canyon before plunging off "Hidden Haven Falls" into Parowan Canyon. The 65-foot waterfall is best in early spring and summer when the creek gushes with water. Later in the summer it dries to a trickle. The waterfall, easily reached from Parowan and I-17, lies in the 892-acre Parowan Canyon Wildlife Management Area.

The hike starts from a large parking lot signed "Hidden Haven and Parowan Canyon Wildlife Management Area" on the east side of UT 143. From the trailhead, the trail follows Parowan Creek to a footbridge and turns east. The second trail section parallels Benson Creek, passing picnic tables and benches before following the rocky creek bed to the base of the waterfall. This final segment requires scrambling over boulders in the creek. Use caution to avoid slipping on loose rock. The creek may be high in spring, so it might be necessary to cross the creek and follow a social

Benson Creek pours over "Hidden Haven Falls" in the Parowan Canyon Wildlife Management Area.

"Hidden Haven Falls"

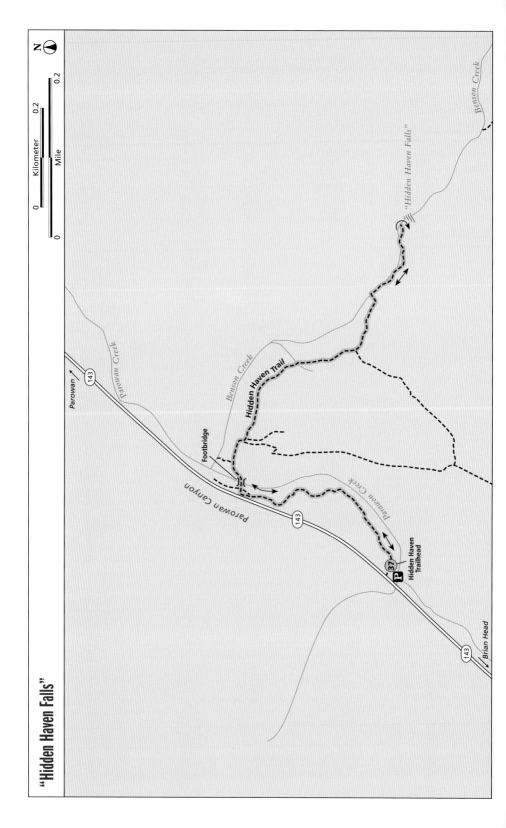

trail through trees on its north bank. The falls area and the creeks are in a potential flash flood area because of burned areas higher in the drainages. Pay attention to the weather to avoid getting caught in a flood.

Miles and Directions

0.0 Start at the Hidden Haven Trailhead, a gap in a log fence on the east side of the large parking lot. Hike through trees and bend left. Hike north on the singletrack trail, paralleling the highway and Parowan Creek, through forest to a sharp right turn.

0.3 Reach a wooden footbridge over Parowan Creek past the right turn (GPS: 37.774923 / -112.838470). Cross the creek and hike east on the trail through a mixed conifer and deciduous forest to an open area with a bench. Continue east on the trail past another bench, two shaded picnic tables, and more benches.

0.6 Reach Benson Creek (GPS: 37.772545 / -112.834246). Go right and hike up the creek bed, scrambling over boulders and occasional logs that may block the creek bed. The creek may be running high in springtime or after heavy rain. Use caution when crossing or hiking in the creek bed during high water.

0.7 The creek bed steepens and is choked with boulders. Continue up the left side of the creek where possible, clambering over boulders.

0.8 Reach the base of "Hidden Haven Falls" below high cliffs (GPS: 37.772010 / -112.832725). Loose rock is everywhere here, so be careful when scrambling over boulders and talus slopes near the waterfall. Return on the trail.

1.6 Arrive back at the trailhead (GPS: 37.772194 / -112.840326).

38 Cascade Falls

A short easy hike descends a trail across the scenic Pink Cliffs to a fenced viewpoint above Cascade Falls, a unique waterfall fed by a creek flowing underground through a lava tube from Navajo Lake.

Start: Cascade Falls Trailhead
Trail: Cascade Falls Trail (#32055)
Difficulty: Easy
Hiking time: About 1 hour
Distance: 1.2 miles out and back
Elevation trailhead to falls viewpoint: 8,925 to 8,875 feet (-50 feet); 90 feet of elevation gain round-trip
Trail surface: Dirt, rocks, wooden steps
Restrictions: Hiking only; no mountain bikes, horses, or motorized vehicles. Do not leave the viewing platform to the waterfall base. The lava tube and creek that feeds the falls are closed because of low oxygen levels, high water, and possible flooding.
Amenities: Vault toilets; large parking lot; viewing platform at falls; benches along trail; services in Cedar City. Duck Creek Visitor Center and Duck Creek Campground are nearby on UT 14.
Maps: *Benchmark Maps:* Page 82 C1; Trails Illustrated #702: Cedar City, Markagunt Plateau; USGS Straight Canyon, Navajo Lake
County: Washington
Land status/contact: Dixie National Forest, Cedar City Ranger District, (435) 865-3200

Finding the trailhead: From Cedar City, drive east on UT 14 for 25 miles to a right turn on FR 30053 toward signed Navajo Lake. Drive 0.3 mile on the paved road and turn left on FR 30370. Drive the dirt road for 1.1 miles to a Y junction. Go right on dirt FR 30054, signed "Cascade Falls." Drive southwest for 1.7 miles through Dry Valley to a large parking lot and the trailhead. GPS: 37.497334 / -112.751767

The Hike

Cascade Falls magically springs from a cave in the Pink Cliffs on the southern edge of the Markagunt Plateau, forming the headwaters of the North Fork of the Virgin River, which flows south into Zion National Park. The 8-foot-high waterfall and long, frothy cascade below create one of Utah's unique geological features. An underground creek feeds the waterfall, flowing through a series of lava tubes and passages before bursting from the cave system through a narrow slit in a ruddy cliff.

The unnamed creek originates in Navajo Lake to the north, which formed when a lava flow dammed a stream. Water escapes the lake through a sinkhole, or depression, caused by the collapse of caves in the Claron Formation and flows south for about a mile through subterranean passageways to the southern edge of the Pink Cliffs. Depending on the level of Navajo Lake, the waterfall fluctuates in volume from a dribble to a

Water trickles through an underground cave system to burst forth at Cascade Falls in the Pink Cliffs.

Cascade Falls

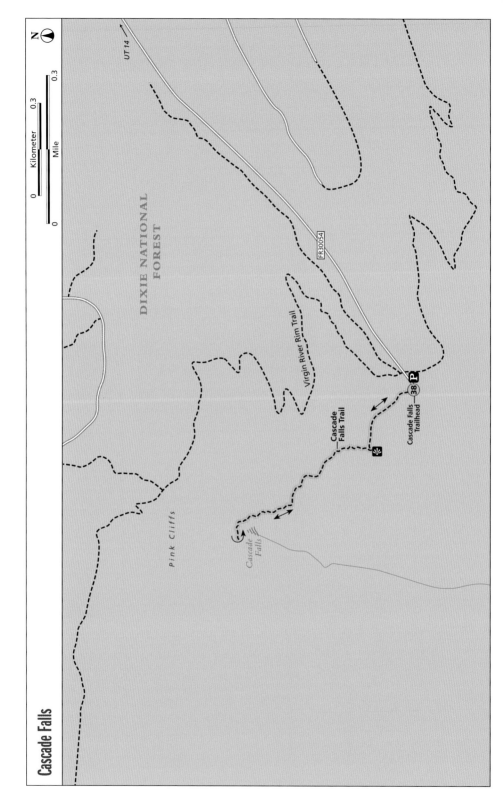

N

Kilometer
0   0.3

Mile
0   0.3

UT 14

DIXIE NATIONAL
FOREST

FR 30054

Virgin River Rim Trail

Cascade
Falls Trail

Pink Cliffs

Cascade
Falls

Cascade Falls
Trailhead

38 P

Cascade Falls hides in the Pink Cliffs, the topmost layers of the Grand Staircase in southern Utah.

deluge. An earthen dam keeps the lake from draining into the sinkhole in dry years, but when water covers the dam, the water drains through the cave system to Cascade Falls.

Reach Cascade Falls by a good trail that gently descends from the trailhead and parking lot to the falls, passing through a forest of pine, spruce, and fir before twisting across steep, dry slopes below cliffs. The Pink Cliffs, the highest step in the Grand Staircase, are formed from the 50-million-year-old Claron Formation, a widespread layer of colorful limestone, sandstone, and conglomerate that forms the distinctive hoodoos, towers, and eroded badlands of nearby Cedar Breaks National Monument and Bryce Canyon National Park. Short pink cliff bands studded with freestanding hoodoos loom above the trail. Partway along the trail is a fenced overlook with majestic views south of distant canyons and rock buttes in Zion National Park.

The best time to see Cascade Falls is early summer when snowmelt swells the creek. The cave system is closed to hikers because of low oxygen levels, high water levels, and possible flooding. Avoid climbing from the viewpoint to the base of the waterfall to avoid damage to eroding rock formations.

Miles and Directions

0.0 Begin the hike at the signed Cascade Falls Trailhead on the west side of the parking lot. Hike northwest on the wide trail through a mixed evergreen forest in the Pink Cliffs.

0.2 Reach a fenced viewpoint with two benches (GPS: 37.498587 / -112.753987). Look southwest across wooded hills and canyons to the Kolob Plateau and deep gorges in Zion National Park. Continue northwest on the narrow trail, gently descending across open slopes and passing below cliffs to the last section up timber steps and boulders.

0.6 Reach a viewing platform above the small waterfall gushing from a hole in a cliff (GPS: 37.502533 / -112.757252). Enjoy the view from the platform but protect the fragile area by not descending to the waterfall. Return up the trail.

1.2 Arrive back at the trailhead (GPS: 37.497334 / -112.751767).

39 Kanarra Creek Waterfalls: "Lower Kanarra Falls," "Kanarra Falls," "Kanarra Boulder Falls," "Upper Kanarra Falls"

Kanarra Creek, north of Zion National Park's Kolob Canyons, offers one of Utah's best waterfall adventures for hikers willing to wade up a cliff-walled tumultuous creek through two slot canyons to four tumbling waterfalls.

Start: Kanarra Creek Trailhead
Trail: Kanarra Creek Trail
Difficulty: Moderate
Hiking time: 3–4 hours
Distance: 3.5 miles out and back
Elevation trailhead to falls viewpoint: 5,620 to 6,190 feet (+570 feet)
Trail surface: Sand, dirt, rocks, water
Restrictions: Fee area; nonrefundable tickets required (buy at kanarrafalls.com/tickets/); 150 people allowed each day. Hiker-only trail; no dogs or bikes. Follow existing trail; pack out trash. Respect wildlife; no carving or graffiti on rocks; no camping or fires on the trail or at the trailhead. Use toilets before hiking to preserve

city watershed; pack out human waste and use a WAG bag, RESTOP, or other portable toilet kit. High flash-flood danger; trail closed in high water. Not recommended for children under 8 years old.
Amenities: Restrooms and water at trailhead; services in Kanarraville and Cedar City
Maps: *Benchmark Maps:* Page 81 B9; Trails Illustrated #702: Cedar City, Markagunt Plateau; USGS Kanarraville
County: Iron
Land status/contact: Bureau of Land Management, Cedar City Field Office, (435) 865-3000; Town of Kanarraville, (435) 590-7490

Finding the trailhead: From Cedar City drive south on I-15 to exit 51 and head south on Old US 91, following signs for Kanarraville. From St. George drive north on I-15 to exit 42. At a stop sign, go right on UT 144/Old US 91 for 0.1 mile. Turn left on Old US 91 and drive north for 4.5 miles to Kanarraville. From the junction of Main and 100 North Streets, drive east on East 100 North for 0.4 mile; turn left into the signed "Kanarra Falls" parking lot and trailhead. GPS: 37.537458 / -113.175631

The Hike

Kanarra Creek, rising on the north slope of flat-topped Kanarra Mountain, drains west through tilted Navajo Sandstone layers in a deeply incised canyon filled with rushing water, mural walls stained black and red, magical slot canyons, and four waterfalls: "Lower Kanarra Falls," "Kanarra Falls," "Kanarra Boulder Falls," and "Upper Kanarra Falls." One of Utah's memorable waterfall hikes follows Kanarra Creek Trail

A metal stepladder allows hiker passage past "Kanarra *Falls," a 12-foot waterfall deep in a slot canyon.*

from the town of Kanarraville to the picturesque whitewater leaps. About half the hike requires wading up the creek in water that ranges from ankle to waist deep. In spring, when the waterfalls run fast, the water is deep, cold, and swift.

The first trail section follows a utility road that accesses Kanarraville's water supply; the wild and scenic second part sticks to the creek, sloshing up the rocky streambed or hugging the banks. Stick to the creek to avoid creating social trails. Two slot canyons, each with a waterfall in its depths, add adventure. A metal stairway climbs "Kanarra Falls," while "Upper Kanarra Falls," the hike's turnaround point, is difficult to bypass without climbing gear. Wear sturdy shoes or canyoneering boots for traction in the creek bed. Sandals work fine, but your feet will get cold. Creek temperatures average 50°F in summer and 30°F in winter. Neoprene socks keep your feet warm, and trekking poles aid your balance.

After the trail became popular on social media, the City of Kanarraville instituted a permit system to lessen human impact and crowding. Daily visitation is limited to 150 hikers a day, who must purchase a nonrefundable permit. Make a reservation at www.kanarrafalls.com. Permits are valid only on specific dates and cannot be resold. Walk-in permits from no-shows are issued later in the day.

Like all Utah slot canyons, Kanarra Creek has a high risk for flash flooding, especially in the afternoon from July through September. Check the daily weather forecast, and do not hike if thunderstorm warnings are issued for the area. When hiking, watch the weather, look for escape routes, and pay attention to rising water levels. The trail may be closed on high-risk days.

Miles and Directions

0.0   Start at the trailhead with an information sign on the southeast side of the parking lot. Hike up timber steps to a closed utility road.

0.05   Reach the road and the trail's permit station. Check in with the attendant and pick up a map. Head north up the utility road, gradually gaining elevation.

0.2   Reach two water towers surrounded by chain-link fencing. The road narrows, bends right, and descends slopes above Kanarra Creek. Pass a vault toilet beside the road before the creek.

0.35   Arrive at Kanarra Creek in the canyon bottom and the first creek crossing (GPS: 37.538167 / -113.170702). Take off your shoes and wade to keep them dry, or plunge into the water, because your shoes will get soaked upstream. Continue east up the canyon on the road on the creek's north bank.

0.75   Reach a junction with a left-pointing arrow. Go left and follow a singletrack trail across the hillside above the creek. The road goes into the creek at the junction. Return to the road and continue east to another creek crossing. Follow the sandy road along the creek's south bank.

1.05   Meet a wire fence and sign designating that you are "Entering Kanarraville Town Administered Lands." This area is part of the town's water supply. The road ends here. Follow a singletrack trail left of the fence to the third creek crossing. From here to the waterfalls, the trail follows the creek, often going up the streambed. Do not follow side trails that deviate

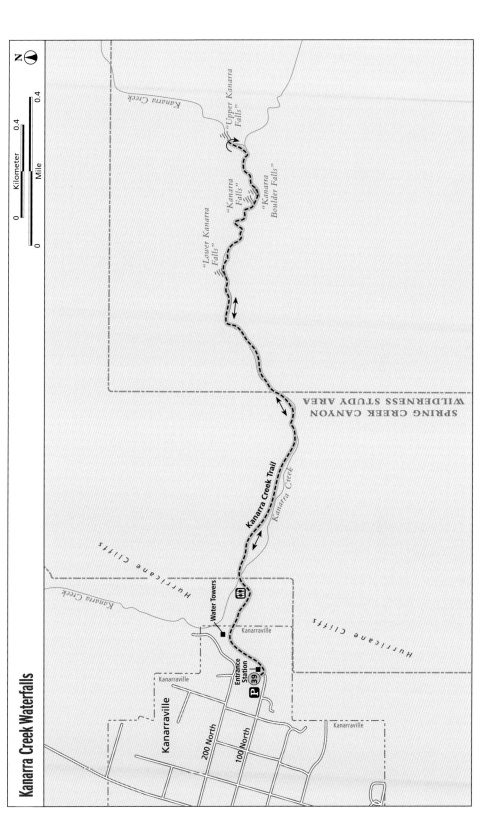

Kanarra Creek Waterfalls

Kanarraville

Kanarraville

Kanarraville

Kanarra Creek

Kanarra Creek

200 North

100 North

P

39

Entrance
Station

Water Towers

Kanarra Creek Trail

Hurricane Cliffs

Hurricane Cliffs

SPRING CREEK CANYON
WILDERNESS STUDY AREA

Kanarra Creek

Kanarra Creek

"Lower Kanarra
Falls"

"Kanarra
Falls"

"Kanarra
Boulder Falls"

"Upper Kanarra
Falls"

N

Kilometer

0   0.4

0   0.4
Mile

"Lower Kanarra Falls" gushes through tilted boulders in the lower canyon.

from the creek. Pass small cascades until the canyon narrows, with cliffs hemming in the creek. A sign here says, "Stay in the River."

1.25 Reach "Lower Kanarra Falls," a 6-foot waterfall gushing through tilted sandstone slabs (GPS: 37.538731 / -113.156092). Cross the creek below the falls and scramble up rocks on the right bank. Continue up the creek, with cliffs dropping into the water. The trail threads in and out of the creek, following the stony bank or wading up the rushing water.

1.5 After making a bowknot bend, reach the entrance to a slot canyon (GPS: 37.537975 / -113.153069). Wade up the creek, which fills the canyon floor. Trekking poles are useful for balance on slippery stones. When the canyon narrows, listen for the sound of a waterfall around the next corner.

1.54 Arrive at "Kanarra Falls," a 12-foot waterfall pouring through a gap (GPS: 37.537602 / -113.152469). Enjoy the cooling mist and then climb a twenty-step metal staircase to the top of the falls. Walk 75 feet up the creek to the next waterfall.

1.55 Reach "Kanarra Boulder Falls," a 10-foot horsetail waterfall splashing off the left side of a massive boulder. Enjoy the roar, then scramble up a slippery log and boulder to the right of the falls and continue wading up the creek. Follow the twisting canyon past a small two-tier waterfall to another slot.

1.75 Reach the second slot canyon. Continue up the narrow canyon, which has deeper water than the first, to the last waterfall.

1.8 Arrive at "Upper Kanarra Falls" in the slot canyon (GPS: 37.538532 / -113.149529). It is difficult to climb past this waterfall, so turn around and retrace the creek and trail back down the canyon.

3.6 Arrive back at the trailhead (GPS: 37.537458 / -113.175631).

40 "Camp Creek Falls"

Located in Zion National Park's northwest corner, "Camp Creek Falls" pours through a polished notch into a rock-walled amphitheater filled with birdsong and falling water.

Start: Camp Creek Falls Trailhead
Trail: Camp Creek Falls Trail
Difficulty: Easy
Hiking time: About 30 minutes
Distance: 0.3 mile out and back
Elevation trailhead to falls viewpoint: 5,450 to 5,505 feet (+55 feet)
Trail surface: Sand, dirt; rocks in creek bed
Restrictions: Zion National Park regulations apply. No dogs or bikes; follow existing trails; pack out trash.

Amenities: None at trailhead; services in Kanarraville and Cedar City
Maps: *Benchmark Maps:* Page 81 B9; Trails Illustrated #214: Zion National Park; USGS Kanarraville
County: Iron
Land status/contact: Zion National Park, (435) 772-3256

Finding the trailhead: From Cedar City go south from exit 57 (Main Street) on I-15 for 15 miles to exit 42, signed "New Harmony Kanarraville." From St. George drive north from exit 13 (Washington Parkway) for 28.8 miles to exit 42. At a stop sign, go right on UT 144/Old US 91 for 0.1 mile. Turn left on Old US 91 and drive north for 1.7 miles toward Kanarraville. Turn right on 1925 South and drive 400 feet to a T junction. Go left onto Wipishani Lane and drive east, past houses, until it ends at 1775 South. Go right on the dirt road by a field to a turnaround loop at a large tree, 0.5 mile from Old US 91. Park on the loop's south side. The trailhead is at the Zion National Park boundary at a gate in a fence on the southeast corner of the loop. GPS: 37.504136 / -113.196958

The Hike

Camp Creek, rising from springs on the north slopes of 8,726-foot Horse Ranch Mountain, the high point of Zion National Park, drops through a steep canyon to a final plunge as "Camp Creek Falls" off an overhanging cliff. The 70-foot waterfall, which often dries up by August, lies in the far northwest corner of Zion, less than 0.5 mile from the park's boundary. Easily accessed from I-15, a short family-friendly trail leads to "Camp Creek Falls," passing the ruins of an old irrigation system and splashing across the shallow creek to the main event.

Miles and Directions

0.0 Start at the trailhead on the boundary of Zion National Park. Go through a gate (remember to shut it behind you) and hike south through tall sagebrush below steep slopes. Scramble

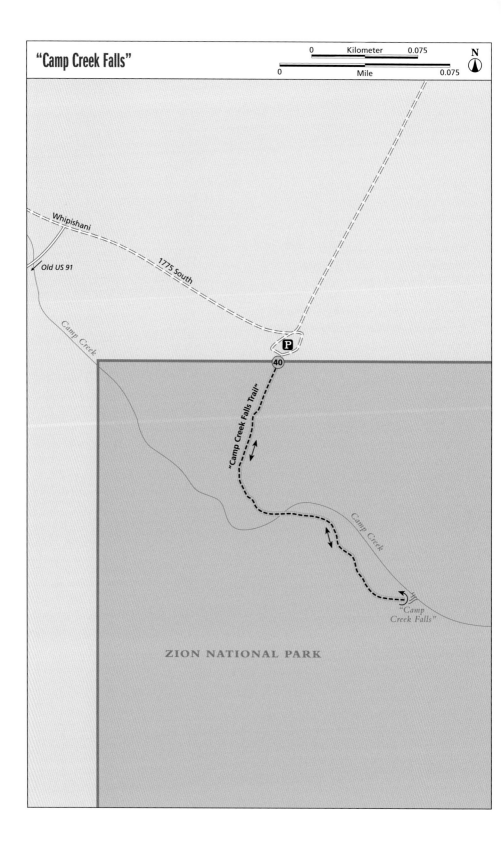

Hiding in Zion National Park's northwest corner, "Camp Creek Falls" drops 70 feet down an overhanging cliff.

up a short hill and follow the trail east to Camp Creek. Cross the creek on rocks and continue east on the trail above the creek toward the waterfall.

0.15 Reach the base of "Camp Creek Falls" in a cliff-lined amphitheater (GPS: 37.502816 / -113.195919). Return on the trail.

0.3 Arrive back at the trailhead (GPS: 37.504136 / -113.196958).

41 Quail Creek Waterfalls: "Quail Creek Falls," "Lower Quail Creek Falls"

Quail Creek uncoils down a sinuous canyon walled with sandstone cliffs to two small waterfalls that pour off ledges into cliff-lined pools at Red Cliffs Recreation Area, northeast of St. George in southwestern Utah.

Start: Red Reef Trailhead
Trail: Red Reef Trail
Difficulty: Easy
Hiking time: About 1 hour
Distance: 1.2 miles out and back
Elevation trailhead to falls viewpoint: 5,450 to 5,505 feet (+55 feet)
Trail surface: Sand, dirt, rocks, slickrock
Restrictions: Day-use fee charged. No dogs or bikes. Follow existing trail; pack out trash.

Amenities: Restrooms; drinking water; Red Cliffs Campground; services in St. George
Maps: Benchmark Maps: Page 81 E7; Trails Illustrated #715: St. George, Pine Valley Mountain; USGS Harrisburg Junction
County: Washington
Land status/contact: Bureau of Land Management, St. George Field Office, (435) 688-3200

Finding the trailhead: From St. George, drive north on I-15 to exit 22. At a T junction, turn right on Old US 91 and drive southwest, paralleling the interstate, for 1.9 miles through Harrisburg to a signed right turn to Red Cliffs Recreation Area. Go right here on West Red Cliffs Campground Road and drive beneath I-15 through two one-lane tunnels to a T junction. Turn left and drive 1.6 miles to Red Reef Trailhead, three parking lots, and Red Cliffs Campground. The trailhead is on the northwest side of the loop at the road's end. GPS: 37.224517 / -113.406356

From Cedar City, drive south on I-15 to exit 23. At a T junction with Silver Reef Road, go left under the interstate and turn right onto North Main Street/UT 228. Drive southwest for 3.5 miles, passing through Leeds, where the road turns into Old US 91, to the right turn to Red Cliff Recreation Area.

The Hike

Sprawling across 44,724 acres north of St. George, Red Cliffs National Conservation Area protects a wide swath of pristine desert ecosystems, cliff-lined canyons, sandstone cliffs, and wildlife, including the endangered desert tortoise. Red Cliffs Recreation Area, tucked into the conservation area's northeast corner, offers a campground, hiking trails, spectacular scenery, and two small waterfalls in cliff-lined Water Canyon. Quail Creek, originating in the rugged Pine Valley Mountains to the north, twists down the sandstone canyon through soaring grottos and narrow slots filled with

"Lower Quail Creek Falls" riffles over sandstone ledges ▶
to a long pool of shimmering water.

Red Reef Trail winds up a canyon past two waterfalls in the Red Reef Recreation Area.

shining pools before splashing over rock benches at "Quail Creek Falls" and "Lower Quail Creek Falls."

Reach the 12-foot-high waterfalls by a short hike on Red Reef Trail, one of the recreation area's best trails. "Lower Quail Creek Falls," dwarfed by surrounding cliffs, riffles through worn potholes before dropping into a long, deep pool that is popular with swimmers and waders on hot days. "Quail Creek Falls," around a bend up Water Canyon, plunges noisily into a deep slickrock bowl. This scenic spot, often busy with other hikers, is a desert oasis with the sweet scent of life-giving water and soaring cliffs. For more adventure, climb the chopped steps to the right of the upper falls and hike farther up the narrow canyon.

Quail Creek usually has flowing water most of the year but sometimes dries up in the scorching summer. Visit from April through June for the best waterfall views. The lower canyon has moderate danger for flash flooding; the upper canyon beyond the second waterfall has elevated risk. Pay attention to the weather and the forecast before entering the canyon. In the event of a flash flood, there are plenty of spots to climb to higher ground in the lower canyon. To avoid severe injuries, do not jump into either of the pools, which are red with silt. The depth of the pools varies, depending on sediment deposited after flooding.

The trail and recreation area are popular. The parking lots have limited spots and quickly fill on weekends, holidays, and during the busy spring and autumn shoulder seasons. Plan to arrive early to nab a parking spot.

Quail Creek Waterfalls

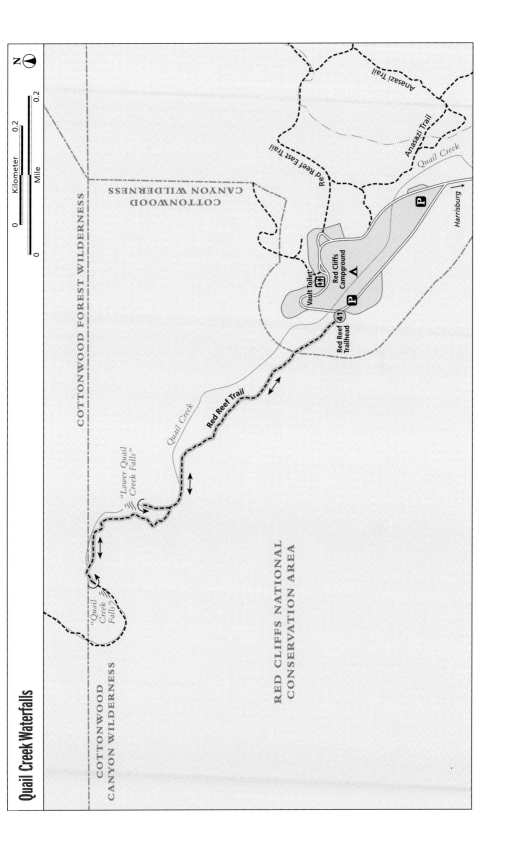

Miles and Directions

0.0 Start at the trailhead on the northwest corner of the one-way loop road through the campground. Hike northwest on the marked trail, crossing sandy hills below cliffs and entering Cottonwood Canyon Wilderness Area. Stay on the trail. The BLM has closed the land along the trail to allow the environment to recover from social trails and human damage.

0.3 The trail reaches a junction and dips to the edge of Quail Creek and tall cottonwood trees. You will return to the trail on the left to continue the hike. Continue straight.

0.35 Reach a long pool encased by sandstone cliffs and the first waterfall, "Lower Quail Creek Falls," at the end of the pool (GPS: 37.228086 / -113.410535). After viewing the falls, return to the trail junction.

0.4 Reach the junction with Red Reef Trail and go right. Climb a hill to a good viewpoint of the canyon, then continue hiking across a bench and descend to Quail Creek.

0.5 At the creek, go left and hike through big boulders below a cliff alongside the creek. Cross it on stones and hike to the edge of a pool below towering sandstone cliffs. Go around the left side of the pool and climb a sandy slab to an upper pool.

0.6 Arrive at the upper pool and "Quail Creek Falls," a small waterfall that drops into the deep pool (GPS: 37.228994 / -113.412259). Chopped steps lead up the sandstone slab to the right of the waterfall to the falls' top and an upper slickrock canyon. Usually, a length of knotted rope hangs over the steps to make it safer. After enjoying this desert oasis, return on the trail.

1.2 Arrive back at the trailhead (GPS: 37.224517 / -113.406356).

"Quail Creek Falls" pours over slickrock into a deep plunge pool.

42 Emerald Pools Waterfalls: "Lower Emerald Pools Falls," "Upper Emerald Pools Falls"

One of Zion National Park's iconic hikes explores two waterfalls at Lower Emerald Pools and a tall seasonal waterfall above Upper Emerald Pools on the three Emerald Pools Trails, in the heart of Zion Canyon.

Start: Emerald Pools Trailhead at Zion Canyon Scenic Drive
Trails: Lower Emerald Pools Trail, Middle Emerald Pools Trail, Upper Emerald Pools Trail
Difficulty: Moderate
Hiking time: 2–3 hours
Distance: 2.1-mile lollipop loop
Elevation trailhead to falls viewpoint: 4,270 to 4,605 feet at Upper Emerald Pools (+335 feet)
Trail surface: Dirt, sand, rocks, slickrock
Restrictions: National park regulations apply. Hikers only. Pack out trash. No swimming or wading in pools or creek. Do not take plants, rocks, and other objects; do not build rock cairns. Follow Leave No Trace principles.
Amenities: Restrooms and water at shuttle stop; none on hike; services in Springdale
Maps: *Benchmark Maps:* Page 81 E11; Trails Illustrated #214: Zion National Park; USGS Temple of Sinawava
County: Washington
Land status/contact: Zion National Park, (435) 772-3256

Finding the trailhead: From the Zion National Park south entrance station, drive north on Zion-Mount Carmel Hwy./UT 9 for 300 feet. Turn right to the Zion Canyon Visitor Center, and park in one of the large lots near the center. Walk to shuttle stop #1 and ride the shuttle up Zion Canyon to stop #5 at Zion Lodge. From the south end of the shuttle lot, reach the Emerald Pools Trailhead by hiking south on the paved Pathways Trail, following signs for Emerald Pools Trail. Keep right at three junctions and after 0.1 mile reach paved Zion Canyon Scenic Drive. Cross the road at a crosswalk to the start of Emerald Pools Trail (GPS: 37.250949 / -112.957997). After hiking the loop, return on Pathways Trail and reboard the shuttle to ride back to the visitor center.

The Zion shuttle system operates daily from March through November. In summer the first shuttle leaves the visitor center at 6 a.m. and the last shuttle leaves stop #9 at 8:15 p.m. Find more information at the park website.

The Hike

Two deep fractures—Behunin Canyon and Heaps Canyon—drain the east and west flanks of 7,060-foot Castle Dome on the West Rim of Zion Canyon, collecting

"Lower Emerald Pools Falls" pounds broken rock on the edge of Lower Emerald Pools.

rainwater and snowmelt that pours down waterfalls in a cliff-walled amphitheater. "Upper Emerald Pools Falls" runs seasonally, usually during spring runoff and after heavy summer thunderstorms, from Heaps Canyon, displaying a spectacular 300-foot waterfall. "Lower Emerald Pools Falls" free-falls in two streams off the lip of an over-hanging 80-foot-high cliff into Lower Emerald Pools. The waterfall runs year-round, but the best viewing is in spring or after rainstorms.

The three Emerald Pools trails—Lower Emerald Pools, Middle Emerald Pools, and Upper Emerald Pools Trails—reach the pools and waterfalls. The lower trail is most popular, with a paved surface and 69 feet of elevation gain. Folks do it as an easy out-and-back hike. The lower trail climbs to a junction with the middle trail, which threads across slickrock above the lower waterfalls and then descends across steep slopes to the river and trailhead. The upper trail leaves the middle trail and climbs almost 0.25 mile, gaining 200, to the upper pool and its seasonal waterfall.

The hike, one of Zion's most popular, sees many visitors. Follow commonsense rules to preserve the unique ecosystems at the pools and waterfalls and lessen human impact. These include staying on the trail; not wading in the pools or creeks; not crossing the creeks at the middle pools in high water (you risk being washed over the cliff); staying behind chains and fences; and following Leave No Trace principles.

Miles and Directions

0.0 Start at the Emerald Pools Trailhead on the west side of Zion Canyon Scenic Drive and hike west on the trail to a footbridge over the Virgin River.

0.1 Reach a T junction and go right. Hike north on the paved Lower Emerald Pools Trail across slopes on the western side of the river and then bending northwest and gently climbing toward an overhanging cliff.

0.6 Arrive beneath the overhanging cliff at Lower Emerald Pool and two streaming waterfalls that pour off the lip above into the pool (GPS: 37.257017 / -112.962705). The trail passes below the cliff, with spring-fed hanging gardens above. Depending on the season and rainfall, the trail may be wet. Continue under the arching cliff and ascend the path below its north side.

0.65 Reach a viewpoint at the cliff's north end and go right on the dirt trail. Follow the trail up right and pass between two giant boulders.

0.7 Reach a junction at the north side of the boulders. Go left on Middle Emerald Pools Trail. The right turn is Kayenta Trail, which heads northeast to shuttle stop #6. Walk around the boulders and dip across a slickrock drainage to the next junction.

0.75 Reach a junction with Upper Emerald Pools Trail (GPS: 37.257587 / -112.962653). Go right on the trail and hike uphill.

0.95 Arrive at Upper Emerald Pools and a seasonal waterfall at the trail's end (GPS: 37.257440 / -112.966411). Relax in the shade and then return down the trail.

1.15 Reach the junction with Middle Emerald Pools Trail. Turn right and walk south on slickrock.

A stream of "Lower Emerald Pools Falls" free-falls ▶
from a cliff below Lady Mountain's north face.

Emerald Pools Waterfalls

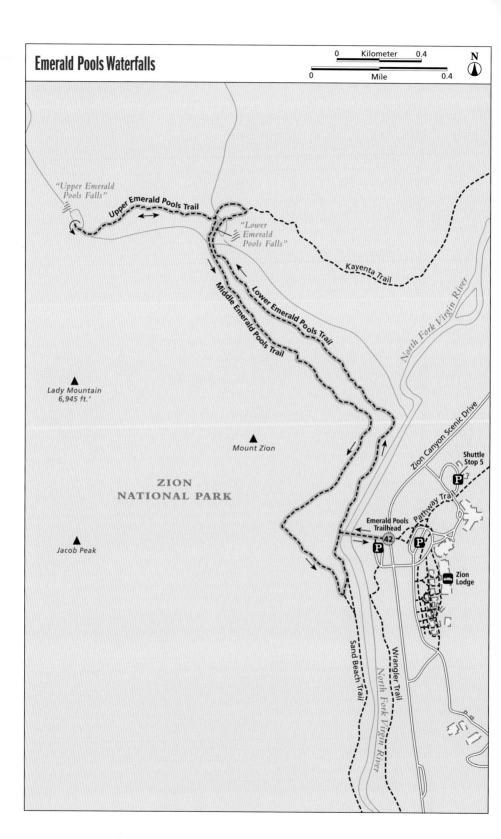

0 Kilometer 0.4

0 Mile 0.4

N

"Upper Emerald Pools Falls"

Upper Emerald Pools Trail

"Lower Emerald Pools Falls"

Kayenta Trail

Lower Emerald Pools Trail

Middle Emerald Pools Trail

North Fork Virgin River

Lady Mountain
6,945 ft.'

Mount Zion

ZION
NATIONAL PARK

Zion Canyon Scenic Drive

Shuttle
Stop 5

P

Pathway Trail

Emerald Pools
Trailhead

42

P

P

Zion
Lodge

Jacob Peak

Sand Beach Trail

Wrangler Trail

North Fork Virgin River

Rainwater fills "Upper Emerald Pools Falls," an ephemeral waterfall that flows after storms. COURTESY OF STUART SEEGER/WIKIMEDIA COMMONS

1.3 Reach Middle Emerald Pools (GPS: 37.257131 / -112.962824), a perfect rest stop with shade and shallow glassy pools that drain off the nearby cliff edge, free-falling down to Lower Emerald Pools. Continue south on the trail, passing views of Zion Canyon and the river.

2.0 Return to the bridge and the first junction. Go right across the footbridge.

2.1 Arrive back at the trailhead (GPS: 37.250949 / -112.957997). Return on the Pathways Trail back to shuttle stop #5.

43 "Lower Pine Creek Falls"

Pouring over a sandstone cliff, two-tiered "Lower Pine Creek Falls" offers a quiet respite from busy Zion Canyon with its splashing water and broad pool filling an amphitheater walled by overhanging cliffs.

Start: Pine Creek Trailhead
Trail: Pine Creek Trail
Difficulty: Moderate
Hiking time: About 1 hour
Distance: 0.6 mile out and back
Elevation trailhead to falls viewpoint: 4,105 to 4,150 feet (+45 feet)
Trail surface: Sand, dirt; rocks in creek bed
Restrictions: National park regulations apply. No dogs or bikes. Park in designated pullout at trailhead. Follow existing trail. Pack out trash; dispose of human waste properly and use a

WAG bag, RESTOP, or other portable toilet kit. Do not build cairns or dams in creek. Do not scratch, paint, or damage rock surfaces. Follow Leave No Trace principles.
Amenities: None at trailhead; campgrounds nearby; services in Springdale
Maps: Benchmark Maps: Page 81 E11; Trails Illustrated #214: Zion National Park; USGS Springdale East
County: Washington
Land status/contact: Zion National Park, (435) 772-3256

Finding the trailhead: From the Zion National Park south entrance station, drive north on Zion-Mount Carmel Hwy./UT 9 for 1.9 miles, passing turns for the visitor center, campgrounds, and the left turn for Zion Canyon Scenic Drive (closed most of the year), to the first switchback. Park in an unnamed pullout on the left (east) side of the highway before Pine Creek Bridge. The trailhead is on the east side of the parking strip (GPS: 37.216611 / -112.965490). The parking lot is 9.4 miles west of the park's east entrance station.

The Hike

Pine Creek, a perennial stream that originates on a high plateau by Deertrap Mountain to the east, twists through a dramatic slot canyon by the Great Arch before tumbling down a boulder-strewn canyon to a 15-foot leap at "Lower Pine Creek Falls."

Pine Creek Trail, beginning on the Zion–Mount Carmel Highway, offers a short, moderate hike that rambles over boulders and short cliffs to the scenic waterfall. Depending on water levels, the hike can be tricky, requiring scrambling over sandy boulders or wading through deep pools. The last section of the trail can be hard to find, but keep to the right side of the creek and work your way up the canyon to this lovely waterfall in a cliff-lined amphitheater.

Like all the waterfalls in Utah's desert canyons, pay attention to the weather before hiking to "Lower Pine Creek Falls." Flash floods from heavy rain farther up the drainage can rampage down the canyon, causing dangerous situations.

"Lower Pine Creek Falls" leaps over two sandstone benches to a gleaming plunge pool. ▶

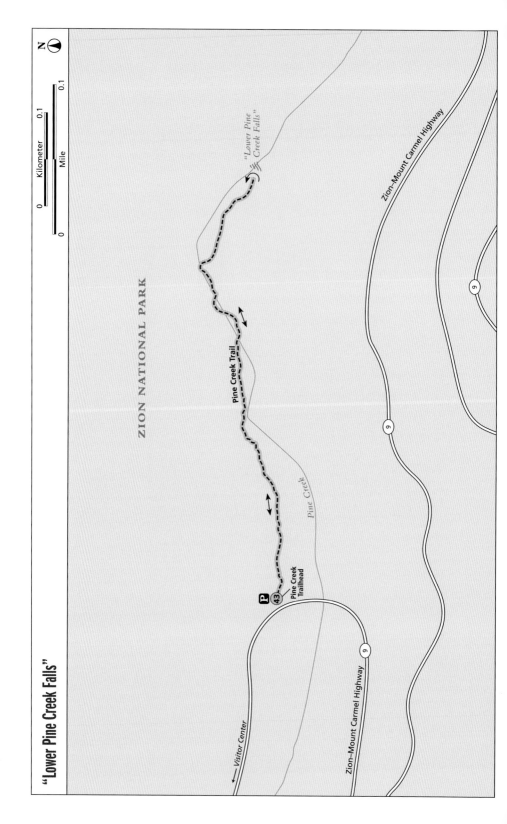

"Lower Pine Creek Falls"

ZION NATIONAL PARK

Pine Creek Trail

Pine Creek

"Lower Pine Creek Falls"

Pine Creek Trailhead

43

P

Visitor Center

Zion–Mount Carmel Highway

Zion–Mount Carmel Highway

Zion–Mount Carmel Highway

9

9

9

N

0   Kilometer   0.1

0   Mile   0.1

Pine Creek reflects sky and stone in the canyon below "Lower Pine Creek Falls."

Miles and Directions

0.0   From the trailhead, hike east on a sandy unmarked trail, keeping left at a junction, to a group of cottonwoods and Pine Creek. Follow the trail north of the creek and pass beneath a cliff. Eventually the canyon pinches down and a cliff rises to the right above the creek.

0.2   Just before reaching a deep pool encased by low cliffs, scramble up right over boulders and climb a short groove up a sandstone cliff to a ledge below the main cliff. Hike a trail above cliffs and a deep pool below. Continue hiking beside the cliff to a boulder leaning against the cliff. Climb through a tunnel between the boulder and cliff (GPS: 37.217011 / -112.960698). To avoid the short climb, it is possible to scramble across boulders on the pool's right side, but they are often sandy, or wade the pool in low water.

0.3   Reach a sandbar and pool below "Lower Pine Creek Falls" (GPS: 37.216870 / -112.960450). After enjoying the dashing waterfall, return down the trail.

0.6   Arrive back at the trailhead (GPS: 37.216611 / -112.965490).

44 "Mystery Falls"

The Narrows of the Virgin River in Zion Canyon offers one of Zion National Park's best easy slot canyon hikes, culminating at 110-foot "Mystery Falls," which pours directly into the river.

Start: Riverside Walk Trailhead at shuttle stop #9
Trails: Riverside Walk, Bottom Up Narrows
Difficulty: Moderate
Hiking time: 2–3 hours
Distance: 4.0 miles out and back
Elevation trailhead to falls viewpoint: 4,420 to 4,505 feet (+85 feet)
Trail surface: Paved, sand, rocks, water
Restrictions: National park regulations apply. Day-use fee; permits not required. Wilderness rules apply. Hikers only; group size limited to 12; stay in watercourse to protect vegetation. No upstream travel beyond Big Spring; inflatable tubes not allowed. Pack out trash; carry out human waste (use RESTOP or WAG bags)

and toilet paper. Do not take plants, rocks, and other objects; do not build rock cairns. Health advisories related to toxic cyanobacteria. Narrows closed when Virgin River flow is above 150 cubic feet per second (cfs). High flash-flood potential; check weather before hiking. Follow Leave No Trace principles.
Amenities: Restrooms and water at trailhead; none on hike; services in Springdale
Maps: *Benchmark Maps:* Page 81 E10–11; Trails Illustrated #214: Zion National Park; USGS Temple of Sinawava
County: Washington
Land status/contact: Zion National Park, (435) 772-3256

Finding the trailhead: From the Zion National Park south entrance station, drive north on Zion-Mount Carmel Highway/UT 9 for 300 feet and turn right to the Zion Canyon Visitor Center. Park in one of the large lots near the center and walk to shuttle stop #1. Ride the shuttle up Zion Canyon to stop #9, Temple of Sinawava, the end of the route. The trailhead is at the shuttle stop (GPS: 37.285260 / -112.947696). After hiking to "Mystery Falls," reboard the shuttle here to ride back to the visitor center.

The Zion shuttle system operates daily from March through November. In summer the first shuttle leaves the visitor center at 6 a.m. and the last shuttle leaves stop #9 at 8:15 p.m. Find more information at the park website.

The Hike

One of Zion's most dramatic waterfalls, "Mystery Falls" is a 110-foot ribbon waterfall that slides over a cliff below Mystery Canyon into The Narrows, a 16-mile-long slot canyon floored by the Virgin River. A hike from the Temple of Sinawava shuttle stop up the paved Riverside Walk and then through the twisting Narrows gorge, which is less than 20 feet wide in places, to "Mystery Falls" is an unforgettable experience.

Hiking up The Narrows is fun, but it is also a serious hike, since you will be wading up the river for the last 0.3 mile to the waterfall. The water depth ranges from

Hikers wade up the Virgin River to "Mystery Falls" in the heart of The Narrows.

ankle deep to waist deep, depending on river levels. While the canyon closes to all hikers if the river flow is above 150 cubic feet per second (cfs), usually in spring and after heavy thunderstorms, expect serious hiking conditions at other times. If the river is running over 70 cfs, plan on difficult walking on slippery rocks and chest-deep pools. If it is below 70 cfs, expect waist-deep pools and knee-deep crossings.

Hikers in The Narrows are at an elevated risk of flash flooding. Pay attention to the weather, and do not enter the canyon if there is a possibility of thunderstorms in the drainage basin above the river. Ask at the visitor center for current conditions and flood advisories.

Wear closed-toe shoes and use a hiking stick or trekking poles for balance. Outfitters in Springdale rent canyoneering shoes and neoprene socks. The National Park Service recommends not wearing sandals or going barefoot, which can result in crushed toes and sprained ankles. The Narrows canyon is cool, breezy, and usually in shadow, even on scorching summer days, since little sunlight reaches the river. Wear synthetic clothes that dry quickly when wet, and bring extra clothing and layers in a waterproof bag. Bring waterproof zip baggies to stash your camera and valuables if you need to wade in deep pools.

Experienced hikers can continue up The Narrows from "Mystery Falls" to see a couple more waterfalls. The next stop is a 10-foot waterfall in Orderville Canyon. Wade up the river for another 1.3 miles to Orderville Canyon on the right. Hike up Orderville's narrow slot canyon for about 0.25 mile to "Veiled Falls," which blocks the canyon. Hikers are not allowed past the waterfall. Return to the main canyon, then continue

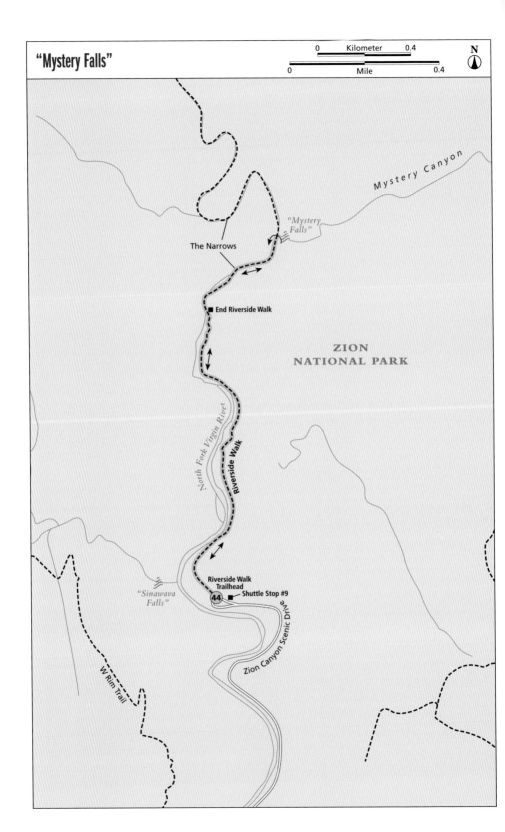

"Mystery Falls"

0   Kilometer   0.4
0   Mile   0.4

N

Mystery Canyon

"Mystery Falls"

The Narrows

End Riverside Walk

ZION
NATIONAL PARK

North Fork Virgin River

Riverside Walk

"Sinawava Falls"

Riverside Walk Trailhead
44   Shuttle Stop #9

Zion Canyon Scenic Drive

W Rim Trail

"Mystery Falls," a 110-foot ribbon waterfall, slides down a steep slab to the Virgin River.

up a spectacular section of The Narrows to reach Big Spring at 4.7 miles. Water gushes from a spring here, forming small waterfalls surrounded by lush vegetation. All upstream hikers must turn around at Big Spring and return to the trailhead.

"Sinawava Falls," across the river from the trailhead and shuttle stop, is one of Zion's most dramatic waterfalls when it runs during spring snowmelt and after thunderstorms. The ephemeral waterfall free-falls about 750 feet from a deep slot canyon on the rim to its rocky base.

Miles and Directions

0.0 Begin at the Riverside Walk Trailhead at shuttle stop #9. Restrooms and a water fill-up station are by the trailhead. Walk north on the paved trail on the east bank of the Virgin River.

1.1 Reach the end of Riverside Walk and start wading up the Virgin River into The Narrows. Depending on water levels, the water ranges from ankle deep to knee or even waist deep.

1.4 Reach the base of "Mystery Falls" on the right (east) canyon wall (GPS: 37.299236 / -112.944547). This is the turnaround point for this hike. Continue up the canyon to see the small falls in Orderville Canyon at 2.7 miles and the small waterfalls at Big Spring at 4.7 miles. From "Mystery Falls," wade back down the river through The Narrows.

1.7 Reach Riverside Walk and follow the paved trail back to the shuttle stop.

2.8 Arrive back at the trailhead (GPS: GPS: 37.285260 / -112.947696).

45 Water Canyon Waterfalls: "Lower Water Canyon Falls," "Middle Water Canyon Falls," "Upper Water Canyon Falls"

Water Canyon, one of southwestern Utah's hidden gems, offers three scenic waterfalls tucked into a narrow canyon filled with the sound of falling water and surrounded by soaring sandstone cliffs.

Start: Water Canyon Trailhead
Trail: Water Canyon Trail
Difficulty: Moderate
Hiking time: About 2 hours
Distance: 2.0 miles out and back
Elevation trailhead to upper falls viewpoint: 5,220 to 5,725 feet (+505 feet)
Trail surface: Sand, dirt, rocks, slickrock
Restrictions: Moderate flash-flood risk in narrow canyon; no camping along trail.

Amenities: Vault toilets; information kiosk; services in Hildale
Maps: *Benchmark Maps:* Page 81 G11; Trails Illustrated #214: Zion National Park; USGS Hilldale
County: Washington
Land status/contact: Bureau of Land Management, St. George Field Office, (435) 688-3200

Finding the trailhead: From St. George, drive north on I-15 and take exit 16 toward Hurricane on UT 9. Drive 9.6 miles east on UT 9 to Main Street in Hurricane and turn right (south) for UT 59. Drive 0.1 mile south on Main Street and turn left on UT 59/East 100 South. Drive southeast for 21.9 miles to Hildale and turn left on Utah Avenue. Continue 2.1 miles east on Utah Avenue, which bends left (north) and becomes Canyon Street. Continue 0.9 mile north on Canyon Street and turn right onto Water Canyon Road. Follow the dirt road, which becomes rough and narrow, for 1.8 miles to the Water Canyon Trailhead and a parking lot at the road's end. (Note: The road may be impassable in wet and muddy conditions.) The trailhead is on the northwest side of the parking lot. GPS: 37.038043 / -112.955427

The Hike

Water Canyon, a deep defile sliced into the Vermillion Cliffs on the southeast side of huge Canaan Mountain, offers three waterfalls—"Lower Water Canyon Falls," "Middle Water Canyon Falls," and "Upper Water Canyon Falls"—in a narrow gap between towering cliffs. More waterfalls tuck in the higher canyon, accessible only to skilled canyoneers.

Fed by a permanent spring-fed creek (it may dry up in hot summers), the three falls plunge and riffle over stone ledges before dashing down a steep, boulder-filled

"Middle Water Canyon Falls" plunges off a cliff from a slot canyon. ▶

Shining pools, hanging gardens, and shady trees fill a verdant gap in Water Canyon.

drainage to the trailhead. Besides pouring over the waterfalls, the creek pools on slickrock slabs and runs through polished rock channels, forming a magical desert oasis. In the arid environment, water provides life for hanging gardens of ferns and flowers on moist cliffs, fills the narrow passages with birdsong, and slakes the thirst of animals.

Beginning at a trailhead north of Hildale and the Arizona border, the Water Canyon Trail steadily climbs sandy slopes above the unnamed creek. Old junipers provide pockets of shade, but bring water or sports drinks, wear a hat, and use sunscreen on sunny days. While most visitors hike in summer's blazing heat, the best time to visit are the shoulder seasons of spring and autumn. The lower canyon has a moderate risk of flash flooding, especially during the July and August monsoon season. Pay attention to the weather on Canaan Mountain, and retreat from the slot canyon if thunderstorms are brewing.

Miles and Directions

0.0 Start at the Water Canyon Trailhead, go through a gate, and follow the sandy trail northwest on the west bank of an unnamed creek. Follow the trail as it steadily climbs boulder-strewn slopes below towering Wingate Sandstone cliffs, heading toward an obvious deep gash between cliffs at the head of the canyon. Look up right to the rim on the canyon's opposite side to spot Water Canyon Arch. The trail finally reaches a high point next to the cliff and descends sandy slopes into a narrow sandstone grotto floored with sand, pools of water, and huge boulders.

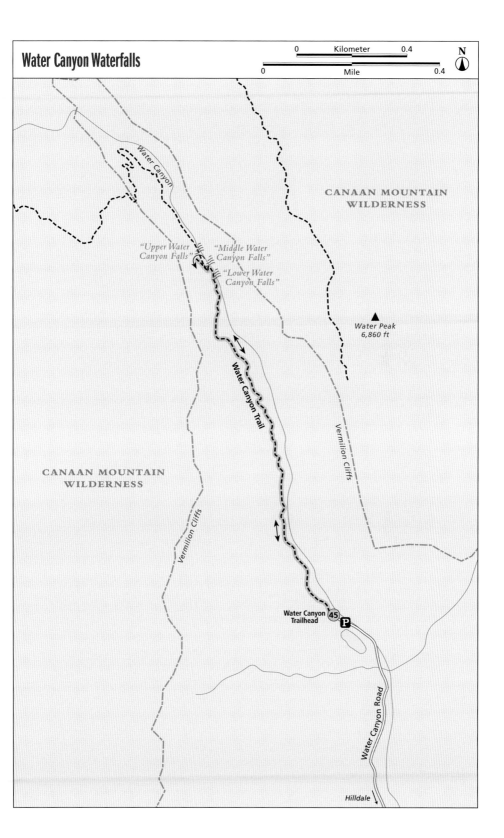

Water Canyon Waterfalls

0
Kilometer
0.4

0
Mile
0.4

N

Water Canyon

CANAAN MOUNTAIN
WILDERNESS

"Upper Water
Canyon Falls"

"Middle Water
Canyon Falls"

"Lower Water
Canyon Falls"

Water Peak
6,860 ft

Water Canyon Trail

CANAAN MOUNTAIN
WILDERNESS

Vermilion Cliffs

Vermilion Cliffs

Water Canyon
Trailhead

45

P

Water Canyon Road

Hildale

"Upper Water Canyon Falls" forms a misty veil of falling water in a narrow chamber.

0.95 Reach the first waterfall, "Lower Water Canyon Falls," a cascade over bedrock in a narrow slot, at the end of the grotto (GPS: 37.049354 / -112.960533). Scramble up the waterfall's left side to a higher opening surrounded by towering cliffs.

0.97 Arrive at the second waterfall, "Middle Water Canyon Falls," a gorgeous 40-foot falls that plunges off a rounded cliff edge into the narrow opening. Continue to the third falls by hiking left from the second falls on a sandstone bench. Go right and follow the trail across a ledge system, then downclimb right into a narrow slot above the second waterfall.

1.0 Wade through the slot into a narrow alcove with the third waterfall, "Upper Water Canyon Falls," plummeting almost 100 feet into the rock-walled chamber (GPS: 37.049824 / -112.961255). This is the turnaround point of the hike, but the rough trail continues up Canaan Mountain, climbing above Water Canyon and looking down at more waterfalls in its upper slot. After enjoying this magical place, return down the trail.

2.0 Arrive back at the trailhead (GPS: 37.038043 / -112.955427).

Appendix

CAMPGROUNDS
Recreation.gov
(877) 444-6777 (reservations)
recreation.gov

NATIONAL PARKS AND MONUMENTS
Bryce Canyon National Park
PO Box 640201
Bryce, UT 84764
(435) 834-5322
nps.gov/brca/

Capitol Reef National Park
HC 70, Box 15
Torrey, UT 84775
(435) 425-3791
nps.gov/care/

Dinosaur National Monument
4545 Hwy. 40
Dinosaur, CO 81610
(435) 781-7700
nps.gov/dino/

Grand Staircase-Escalante National Monument
669 S Hwy. 89A
Kanab, UT 84741
(435) 644-1200
blm.gov/programs/national-conservation-lands/utah/grand-staircase-escalante
-national-monument

Grand Staircase-Escalante National Monument
Escalante Interagency Visitor Center
755 W Main St.
Escalante, UT 84726
(435) 826-5499
blm.gov/visit/escalante-interagency-visitor-center

National Parks Pass
nps.gov/planyourvisit/passes.htm
usparkpass.com

Zion National Park
1 Zion Park Blvd.
Springdale, UT 84767
(435) 772-3256
nps.gov/zion/

NATIONAL FORESTS

Dixie National Forest
Cedar City Ranger District
820 N Main St.
Cedar City, UT 84721-7769
(435) 865-3200
fs.usda.gov/recarea/dixie/recarea/?recid=24840

Fishlake National Forest
Beaver Ranger District
575 S Main St.
Beaver, UT 84713
(435) 438-2436
fs.usda.gov/detail/fishlake/about-forest/districts/?cid=STELPRDB5108819

Fishlake National Forest
Fremont Ranger District
138 S Main St.
PO Box 129
Loa, UT 84747
(435) 836-2800
fs.usda.gov/detail/fishlake/about-forest/districts/?cid=FSM9_019910

Manti–La Sal National Forest
Sanpete Ranger District
540 N Main St.
Ephraim, UT 84627-1117
(435) 636-3300
fs.usda.gov/mantilasal

Uintah-Wasatch-Cache National Forest
Heber-Kamas Ranger District
50 E Center St.
PO Box 68
Kamas, UT 84036
(435) 783-4338
fs.usda.gov/detail/uwcnf/about-forest/districts/?cid=stelprdb5048485

Uinta-Wasatch-Cache National Forest
Pleasant Grove Ranger District
390 N 100 East
Pleasant Grove, UT 84062
(801) 785-3563
fs.usda.gov/detail/uwcnf/about-forest/districts/?cid=stelprdb5042982

Uintah-Wasatch-Cache National Forest
Salt Lake Ranger District
6944 S 3000 East
Cottonwood Heights, UT 84121
(801) 733-2660
fs.usda.gov/detail/uwcnf/about-forest/districts/?cid=fsem_035528

Uintah-Wasatch-Cache National Forest
Spanish Fork Ranger District
44 W 400 North
Spanish Fork, UT 84660
(801) 798-3571
fs.usda.gov/detail/uwcnf/about-forest/districts/?cid=stelprdb5042983

BUREAU OF LAND MANAGEMENT
Cedar City Field Office
176 E D. L. Sargent Drive
Cedar City, UT 84721
(435) 865-3000
blm.gov/office/cedar-city-field-office

Moab Field Office
82 E Dogwood Ave.
Moab, UT 84532
(435) 259-2100
blm.gov/office/moab-field-office

Price Field Office
125 S 600 West
Price, UT 84501
(435) 636-3600
blm.gov/office/price-field-office

Red Cliffs National Conservation Area
345 E Riverside Dr.
St. George, UT 84790
(435) 688-3200
blm.gov/programs/national-conservation-lands/utah/red-cliffs-nca

St. George Field Office
345 E Riverside Dr.
St. George, UT 84790
(435) 688-3200
blm.gov/office/st-george-field-office

WILDLIFE AREAS
Utah Division of Wildlife Resources (Southern Region)
Parowan Canyon Wildlife Management Area
1470 N Airport Rd.
Cedar City, UT 84721
(435) 865-6100
wildlife.utah.gov

CITY PARKLANDS
Ogden Trails Network
1875 Monroe Blvd.
Ogden, UT 84401
(801) 629-8214
ogdencity.com/545/Ogden-Trails-Network

Sandy Parks and Recreation
440 E 8680 South
Sandy, UT 84070
(801) 568-2900
sandy.utah.gov/407/Parks-and-Recreation

Town of Kanarraville
40 S Main St.
HC 65, Box 148
Kanarraville, UT 84742
(435) 590-7490
kanarrafalls.com

Utah County Parks and Trails
2855 S State St.
Provo, UT 84606
(801) 851-8600
provo-canyon-parks.weebly.com/bridal-veil-falls.html

Weber County Parks and Recreation
1181 N Fairgrounds Dr.
Ogden, UT 84404
(801) 399-8230
wcparksrec.com/northfork

Hiking Index

THE TEN ESSENTIALS OF HIKING

American Hiking Society

American Hiking Society recommends you pack the "Ten Essentials" every time you head out for a hike. Whether you plan to be gone for a couple of hours or several months, make sure to pack these items. Become familiar with these items and know how to use them.

1. Appropriate Footwear
Happy feet make for pleasant hiking. Think about traction, support, and protection when selecting well-fitting shoes or boots.

2. Navigation
While phones and GPS units are handy, they aren't always reliable in the backcountry; consider carrying a paper map and compass as backups and know how to use them.

3. Water (and a way to purify it)
As a guideline, plan for half a liter of water per hour in moderate temperatures/terrain. Carry enough water for your trip and know where and how to treat water while you're out on the trail.

4. Food
Pack calorie-dense foods to help fuel your hike, and carry an extra portion in case you are out longer than expected.

5. Rain Gear & Dry-Fast Layers
The weatherman is not always right. Dress in layers to adjust to changing weather and activity levels. Wear moisture-wicking clothes and carry a warm hat.

6. Safety Items (light, fire, and a whistle)
Have means to start an emergency fire, signal for help, and see the trail and your map in the dark.

7. First Aid Kit

Supplies to treat illness or injury are only as helpful as your knowledge of how to use them. Take a class to gain the skills needed to administer first aid and CPR.

8. Knife or Multi-Tool

With countless uses, a multi-tool can help with gear repair and first aid.

9. Sun Protection

Sunscreen, sunglasses, and sun-protective clothing should be used in every season regardless of temperature or cloud cover.

10. Shelter

Protection from the elements in the event you are injured or stranded is necessary. A lightweight, inexpensive space blanket is a great option.

Find other helpful resources at AmericanHiking.org/hiking-resources